J⊚KES

JKES

PHILOSOPHICAL THOUGHTS ON JOKING MATTERS

TED COHEN

THE UNIVERSITY OF CHICAGO PRESS ● CHICAGO AND LONDON

The University of Chicago Press, Chicago 60637
The University of Chicago Press, Ltd., London
© 1999 by The University of Chicago
All rights reserved. Published 1999
Paperback edition 2001
08 07 06 05 04 03 02 01   3 4 5

ISBN 0-226-11230-6 (cloth)
ISBN 0-226-11231-4 (paperback)

Library of Congress Cataloging-in-Publication Data

Cohen, Ted.
    Jokes : philosophical thoughts on joking matters /
Ted Cohen.
        p.   cm.
    Includes bibliographical references and index.
    ISBN 0-226-11230-6 (cloth : alk. paper)
    1. Wit and humor—History and criticism.   I. Title.
PN6147.C56   1999
809.7—DC21   99-12810
                                              CIP

For my mother, Shirley Cohen,
a woman of courage and laughter,
who knows and shows that it
sometimes takes courage to laugh

CONTENTS

CONTENTS

ACKNOWLEDGMENTS

A lucky man lives in many communities. My luck has brought me into many in which jokes are some of the currency of intimacy. For nearly twenty years I have had the great fortune to know Joel Snyder, a man who knows and likes jokes, and knows what they are for. Every joke-lover knows, when he hears a good joke, to whom he will go to tell it. I have almost always gone to Snyder. He has been an outstanding appreciator, but his decency, intelligence, and honesty have always led him to let me know when my joke is not funny, not good, in inexcusably bad taste, or too old and worn to be worth hearing again. Some of the jokes in this book may not have passed muster with him, but he has heard them all.

Not all my friends have rich senses of humor, and not all who like humor, like jokes. It is a special treat when one's friendship is amplified by joking, and I have had that treat in many friendships. Some are far flung, like my enduring friendship with Bohdan Dziemidok. In Lublin, in Gdansk, in Krakow, and in Chicago, we have talked a lot of philosophy and a lot of politics, and we have told jokes. His are wonderful, and he has abided mine.

For the past few years my near-daily fare has been a billiards game at noon, and the conversation surrounding that game includes various attempts at wit, including some of the strangest jokes one might imagine. James Lorie reminds us of the stern standard according to which no joke without obscenity is really a joke, and that a really fine joke is fit for any company. The late Raj Bahadur, a man of impeccable taste and dignity, ostensibly insisted on clean, morally upright jokes. And so I learned how to deal with an impossible audience, one containing both Lorie and Bahadur. Nicholas Rudall is far and away the best mimic and dialectician I have known, and he is one of those rare companions with whom one can work on a joke, trying it out, altering it, realizing that the character should be Chinese, not Jewish, and that the task should be to start a restaurant, not to run a tailoring business. Rudall and I have collaborated on more than a few jokes while waiting our turns at the table, enjoying ourselves all the more for knowing that our giggling conversation distracts our opponents as they try to shoot pool. Julian Goldsmith was a mainstay of the game until his health forced him, first, to leave the game, then to leave kibbitzing, and, finally, to spend much of his time at home. While he was in the game, playing and kibbitzing, he was a unique joke-teller and -appreciator, not the least because of his all-purpose Russian-Greek and Cherokee-Jewish accents, and also because of his insatiable interest in every damned thing one might think of. He continues to be an inspiration, mainly through my e-mail, which he clutters, and also by telling me that this book is OK.

Professional meetings, usually held annually, are good for academic and scholarly work, and they are priceless for the opportunity to be with those seldom-seen friends who come knowing that jokes await. I always profit from meetings of the American Society for Aesthetics, but those meetings would be diminished infinitely for me if I did not find Stanley Bates and Tim Gould there. Bates's spontaneously created jokes during lectures we attend are always a threat to get me expelled as I collapse in convulsive whispered laughter, and Gould is an eternal inspiration because of his rich appreciation of rich jokes, and because of his unquenchable need, a need he attributes to his living in Denver, where he blames the local Jewish population for spending its time skiing instead of tending to its proper business, which is to retail jokes.

Sometimes, rarely, one gets a joke that is funny, of course, but that also embodies some profound understanding of things, and when I get a joke like that I go looking for special audiences, and my audience always includes Stanley Cavell, even when I can do no better than leave the joke on his answering machine. It is worth it, for no truly good joke is wasted on Cavell.

There are so many others I could name, those who have done me the blessed favor of laughing at my jokes, and have made me laugh at theirs. I have done my best to name them all, or as many as I can remember in the footnotes that constitute this book's scholarship, and I will leave it at that except for three special people I must mention.

Both my children have tolerated my jokes since they were born. But more. Shoshannah Cohen does me the very great favor of passing on to me jokes she does not care for, knowing me so well that she knows that I will like them, and caring enough for me to give them to me. She teaches me literature, and many other things, and she gives me those jokes. Every father should have a daughter like that.

Amos Cohen has done me the *mitzvah* of deploying his natural concern for depth and meaning to the jokes he comes across, and then instructing me. I hope I am worthy.

Andy Austin Cohen, my wife, is the most remarkably versatile person I have known. She is comfortable with professors and scientists and policemen and judges and lawyers and members of high society and musicians and . . . you name it. And she loves jokes. She takes them from, and tells them to, all those different kinds of people. Many things make a marriage, and we have more than a few, including endless conversation, and some of our conversation is the consideration of jokes with regard to predicting who will like them and who will not. She is very nearly infallible. In other ways, as well.

INTRODUCTION

A PHILOSOPHER ONCE SAID, "Don't take it as a matter of course, but as a remarkable fact, that pictures and fictitious narratives give us pleasure, occupy our minds."[1]

I think we should be struck once again by the fact that there is a kind of story meant to make us laugh. The fact of jokes—the fact that there are such things—is something of note, something worth thinking about.

Jokes are the only kind of humor this book is about, strictly speaking, and by 'jokes' I mean only a few particular kinds of contrivance. I believe that the descriptions I will attempt of these things apply as well to other forms of humor, including comedy. I will say something about how jokes work (at least some of them), why we use jokes, what they achieve, and what their existence may show about those of us who love them. It may be that these remarks would apply to many of the ways in which we make ourselves laugh, but I offer them only as remarks about jokes. Most of the jokes I have in mind are of two kinds. One is the kind of joke that is a very short story— fictional, beginning with a description of people, their things,

1. Ludwig Wittgenstein, *Philosophical Investigations*, Section I, Paragraph 524.

and their actions, and ending with a very concise conclusion (usually a single sentence) called 'the punch line'. Such jokes typically begin with openings like

> **The Pope decides to have a garden made inside the Vatican.**

or

> **A Jew was called to serve in the army.**

or

> **A priest in a small parish in the south of Ireland feared that paganism had appeared among his parishioners.**

The other kind of joke is more obviously formulaic. Examples are lightbulb-changing jokes, and what are called 'ethnic jokes', among others. These jokes typically begin with a question, like

> **How many Christian Scientists does it take to change a lightbulb?**

but they need not, as in

> **A Sikh walked into a travel agency in New Delhi.**

These two kinds of formula jokes exhibit different logical forms, so to speak. One holds the ethnicity constant, and changes the task. For instance,

> **How does an Irishman build a house, drink a Guinness, drive a car?**

The other kind of formula holds the task constant and changes the agent. For instance,

> **How does a Pole or a psychiatrist or a Jewish mother change a lightbulb?**

But sometimes both logical forms are at work.

How many Jewish mothers does it take to change a lightbulb?

may be—probably is—both a lightbulb-changing joke and a Jewish mother joke.

And the distinction may also be blurred between formula jokes and short story jokes. A joke that begins

An Irish golfer hooked his drive into the woods.
When he went to look, he couldn't find his ball, but
he captured a leprechaun.

may be a golf joke, an Irish joke, and a leprechaun joke, all embedded within a short story, with its end a genuine narrative conclusion spoken by the golfer.

Many jokes are usefully thought of as solutions to problems that have been set, and they may well be created in that way. In this respect they bear a faint resemblance to problems of simultaneous equations in elementary algebra. Find x and y, when $x + y = 7$ and $x - y = 3$. Of course there is a technique (in fact a perfectly mechanical one) for solving this problem, but one might dispense with that and simply try to *see* the solution. Thus one tries to answer

How many members of the Spartacist Youth League
does it take to change a lightbulb?

by seeing a way of joining the commonplace characteristics of the Sparts with the requirements of lightbulb-changing.

When it works, this joke will work because its audience brings to the joke its own awareness of certain assumptions about the characteristics of Spartacist Youth League members (and, of course, its knowledge of lightbulb-changing). It is an essential feature of the joke that it not itself contain instruction in the characteristics of Sparts, but that it presume this knowledge in the audience. A great many jokes enjoy this kind of concision, presuming their audiences able to supply a requisite background, and exploiting this background. This fact is a key to understanding the insinuating quality of jokes, a way in which they force their audiences to join in the joke.

If making up a joke were the same as solving an equation, then everyone could do it. Everyone could learn to do it. Some people would be quicker at it than others, and some people would be more reliably accurate, but everyone would be able to do it. But not everyone is able to do it. Nor is everyone able to improve a given joke, say by replacing the Italian-tenor main character with an Israeli pianist.

On the other hand, many who are unable to make up jokes are amused by them and may care for them so much that they seek them out and collect them and tell them to others. And yet there are people who do not care for jokes, and are seldom if ever amused by them.

There is no formula for making up jokes, and not everyone can do it. A joke cannot force everyone to be amused, and some people are unamused by some jokes. Some people are not amused by any jokes. These facts about jokes are interesting, and perhaps surprising. They seem to me exactly as interesting and surprising as the facts that there are no formulas or recipes for making up figures of speech, or for creating works of art, and the facts that not everyone can grasp every figure of speech, that some people don't care for some art, and some people don't much like art at all.

The striking similarities between jokes, figures of speech, and works of art are worth attention, and wonder, but I will pass them over in this book about jokes, except for noting one similarity here, and a few others in later sections, especially when I describe using jokes as devices for inducing intimacy.

Here I note that there is a normal practice of joke-telling that may itself be assumed for purposes of making "second level" jokes, just as normal practices of art-making and art-appreciating make possible a kind of second level art. By "assuming the practice of joke-telling" I do not mean doing so only in order to tell a joke-within-a-joke, although such an embedded joke does play on this background. An example of that is this story, presented to me explicitly as an English joke, which I heard years ago in Alberta:

A man told this joke to a group of acquaintances, including an Englishman.

"A man walked into a saloon, sat at the bar, and ordered a martini. When the drink had been put in front of him, before he could touch it, a monkey that had been sitting on the bar a few yards away walked over to the drink, straddled it, and bent until his genitals were in the drink. In horror the patron said to the bartender, 'Did you see that?'

"'Oh yes,' replied the bartender, 'that was one of the worst things I've seen in this bar.'

"'Well, what are you going to do about it?' demanded the patron.

"'I'm afraid I can't do anything,' said the bartender, 'the monkey belongs to the piano player.'

"The patron immediately strode to the piano and said to the piano player, 'Do you know your monkey dipped his balls in my martini?'

"'No,' said the piano player, 'but if you can hum a few bars I'll pick it up.'"

When the joke was finished, all laughed except the Englishman. When he was asked why he didn't like the joke, he replied that he had not understood it. It was then explained to him that the expression 'Do you know . . . ?' has a special significance for musicians, and then he laughed considerably.

"So now that you understand it, you think it's pretty good?" he was asked.

"Oh my, yes," he replied, "but you do have to know the tune."[2]

Although that joke contains a joke—and a decent one at that—and takes the idea of joke-telling for granted, it does not

2. I learned this story several years ago, after I had delivered a lecture at the University of Lethbridge, in Alberta. I am distressed to have forgotten the name of the Lethbridge professor who told me the story (and he told it very well) during the course of a conversation about the relation of Canada to England.

significantly exploit the joke-telling background. Nor does this one, although it does presuppose at least a minimal acquaintance with normal lightbulb-changing jokes:

> How many surrealists does it take to change a
> lightbulb?
> Fish.

This next joke does play upon a joke-telling background, although it is not simply a joke, but is a kind of limerick-incorporating joke, and also requires of its audience some familiarity with limericks and the problems of constructing and remembering them:

> One day a Church of England reverend is visited in his rectory by one of his parishioners. "Reverend," says the man, "recently I've heard a very amusing story I'd like to tell you, but it's just a bit off-color."
>
> "That's no problem," says the cleric. "For the sake of a good story I don't mind a little ribaldry."
>
> "Good," says the parishioner. "Now I must be careful, because I have some trouble remembering it exactly. I think this is it:
>
>> There once was a young man named Skinner
>> Who had a young lady to dinner.
>> They sat down to dine
>> At a quarter till nine,
>> And by 9:45 it was in her."
>
> "What was in her," asks the churchman, "the dinner?"
>
> "No, Reverend, it was Skinner. Skinner was in her."
>
> "Oh my, yes," says the reverend. "Very amusing."
>
> A few weeks later the reverend is visited by his bishop, to whom the reverend says, "Bishop, one of my flock told me a terribly amusing story that I'd be delighted to tell you if you don't mind its being just a bit lewd."

"Oh no," says the bishop. "It will do nicely if it is amusing."

"Good," says the reverend, "but I must be careful and go slowly, for I sometimes have trouble remembering. I think this is it:

> There once was a young man named Tupper
> Who had a young lady to supper.
> First they had tea
> At a quarter till three,
> And by 3:45 it was up her."

"Up her?" asks the bishop. "What was up her? The supper?"

"No, no, Bishop—actually it was a complete stranger named Skinner."[3]

The stories that most conspicuously play upon joke-telling itself, probably, are what are called 'shaggy dog stories'. The Urexample, I suppose, is this:

> A boy owned a dog that was uncommonly shaggy.
> Many people remarked on its considerable shagginess.
> When the boy learned that there are contests for
> shaggy dogs, he entered his dog, and the dog won first
> place for shagginess in local and regional competitions. The boy entered the dog in ever-larger contests,
> until finally he entered his dog in the world championship for shaggy dogs. When the judges had inspected
> all the competitor dogs, they remarked about the boy's
> dog, "He's not so shaggy."

If this is a joke, then it is a joke in the way in which certain works of Dada and Neo-Dada are art. They play upon a pre-

---

3. Kenneth Northcott favored me with this gem, and he did it perfectly, with just the right tone and accent for the relevant British clergymen. I have discovered that in order to remember it, it is very useful to tell it at least once every few months.

sumed background known to the audience, namely the background of normal joke-telling or art-exhibiting. Thus oriented, the audience approaches this item with expectations that are either simply disappointed or met in an utterly unexpected manner. Thus John Cage's *Four minutes, 33 seconds* is given to an audience expecting to hear audible musical events, and the audience hears no traditional music. The story about the shaggy dog is given to people listening to the narrative and expecting it to culminate in a punch line of a certain kind.

Something of an intermediate case is this story:

In nineteenth-century Russia a young Jew is told he is to be conscripted into the army. So he asks an old Jew for advice.

"There's nothing to worry about," says the old man. "Just go into the army and things will turn out well."

"How can you be sure?" asks the young man.

"Well, when you have joined the army, there are two possibilities—either you will be sent to a combat group, or you won't. If not, then there is nothing to worry about.

"If you are sent to a combat group, then there are two possibilities—either the group will be sent into combat, or it won't. If not, then there is nothing to worry about.

"If the group is sent into combat, then there are two possibilities—either you will be wounded, or you won't. If not, then there is nothing to worry about.

"If you are wounded, then there are two possibilities—either the wound will be mortal, or it won't. If not, then there is nothing to worry about.

"If the wound is mortal, then there are two possibilities—either you will go to hell or you will go to heaven. If you go to heaven, then there is nothing to worry about.

"If you go to hell, then there are two possibilities—either they take bribes or they don't. If they take bribes, there is nothing to worry about.

"Of course they take bribes."[4]

This is not truly a shaggy dog story, because it does have a punch line, and a funny one at that. It is probably more accurately thought of as one of those jokes meant to parody—or represent—Talmudic reasoning, and in that respect it is somewhat like the two-men-going-down-a-chimney joke. But it also has, or nearly has, the abrupt ending and emptiness characteristic of shaggy dog stories, and other joke-like concoctions that play upon the audience's expectation and then thwart it.

An oddity of these stories, these joke-like stories that go nowhere, is that their presumption upon the audience is simultaneously enormous and negligible. It is enormous in that it presupposes an acquaintance with joke-telling in general, and an appreciation of how jokes work; but it is negligible in that it presupposes nothing else, no specific information, no particular dispositions to feel one way or another. I suppose they are conditional jokes (or joke-like), but the condition they presuppose is just joking itself. The background for these jokes is normal joking, and whatever purpose these "meta-jokes" serve, we may ask just what normal joking is for. Only a fool, or one of those who believe in "theories," would presume to say, in general, what the purpose of joking is. I am neither foolish enough to believe in, nor theory-ridden enough to attempt, such a comprehensive result. Of course I will make a few conceptual claims, trying to understand something of the structures of some jokes and their audiences. A philosopher has to say at least a few theoretical words. But I will attempt

4. This joke was told to me a number of years ago by Leo Steinberg. In the interim, however, I am embarrassed to say, I forgot the punch line, a matter of real distress to me because I take pride in my ability to file jokes mentally and then call them up. I was saved by Ms. Paula Molner, a woman of considerable attainments, who undertook to retrieve the joke from her friend Mr. Steinberg, and then gave it back to me.

nothing global or universal; there will be no comprehensive theory of jokes or their purpose, not only because I have no such theory but also because I believe there could be no such theory. I will be saying only that some jokes on some occasions serve some purposes, and the principal ones I will describe are relief from certain oppressions, and the attainment of a very special kind of intimacy. Both achievements are accomplished with specific audiences, the audiences specific to the jokes that generate them. There is a slight ambiguity in the idea of a joke's audience. Those who make up jokes are not always the same as those who tell them.

Joking is a "two-stage" art, like music and theater. Someone must make up the joke, and someone must tell it, and these two jokers need not be the same. Those good at making up jokes are not the same as those good at telling them. Telling a joke well may require specific abilities, like being able to affect an Irish dialect, or it may require a subtle knack, like a sense of timing. This is especially important because some jokes are much more likely to succeed if they are heard than they are if they are read. For instance,

> A Sikh walked into a travel agency in New Delhi, and said to an agent, "I wish to purchase an airplane ticket to the Netherlands. I must go to the Haig-you."
>
> "Oh, you foolish Sikh. Not 'Haig-you'. You mean 'The Hague'."
>
> "I am the customer and you are the clerk," replied the Sikh. "Do as I ask, and hold your tung-you."
>
> "My, my, you really are quite illiterate," laughed the agent. "It is not 'tung-you'. It is 'tongue'."
>
> "Just sell me the ticket, you cheeky fellow. I am not here to arg."[5]

It is not only that the mispronunciations of 'Hague', 'tongue', and 'argue' are more effective if heard, but also that

5. This is one of the first Indian jokes I learned. It was given to me by Akeel Bilgrami.

the joke profits considerably if the teller can affect Indian-accented English in the manner of the late Peter Sellers.

This joke virtually disappears when it is only written:

According to Freud, what comes between fear and sex?

Fünf.[6]

And in fact there is no way to write it correctly. I have written it with 'fear' and 'sex', but I might have used '*vier*' and '*sechs*', and either way, something would have been left out. For a novice German speaker whose native language is English, however, '*vier*' / 'fear' and '*sechs*' / 'sex' are nearly identical when spoken, and that is what makes the joke work.

There are kinds of music-making and acting in which the composition/performance distinction breaks down. These are called, usually, *improvisational* activities. There are multiple jazz performances of a single composition, but there are also jazz undertakings in which there was no antecedent composition, but only on-the-spot improvisation. (It is not entirely unproblematic to call such occasions *performances,* although the word is used of them.) So it is with some joke-making, and these occasions often are group activities. It occurs to one of us to attempt to create a joke, say, about Trent Lott and his curious understanding of religious morality. A first stab is followed by an improvement, then an elaboration, and finally we have produced—

According to Senator Lott, if Ellen DeGeneres were a good Christian, she would have been born a heterosexual man.

6. Cathleen Cavell left this joke for me on my answering machine. It was a perfect way to encounter the joke, for this joke is entirely an auditory matter, and on the answering machine Ms. Cavell was, as Conrad says, only a voice.

2

JOKES ARE CONDITIONAL

WHEN I FIRST WROTE ABOUT JOKES, [7] I thought of dividing them into the pure ones and the conditional ones. A conditional joke is one that can work only with certain audiences, and typically is meant only for those audiences. The audience must supply something in order either to get the joke or to be amused by it. That something is the *condition* on which the success of the joke depends. It is a vital feature of much joking that only a suitably qualified audience—one that can meet the condition—can receive the joke, and the audience often derives an additional satisfaction from knowing this about itself. A pure joke would be universal, would get through to everyone, because it presupposed nothing in the audience.

It now seems clear to me that there is no such thing as a pure joke. It is a kind of ideal, but it doesn't exist. At the very least, the audience will have to understand the language of the joke, and probably much more. But even if all jokes are conditional, it is still useful to note just how strongly conditional a particular joke is, and just what kind of condition is presupposed.

When the background condition involves knowledge or belief, I call the joke *hermetic*. Perhaps all you need to understand

---

7. That was in a short essay, "Jokes," first published in *Pleasure, Preference and Value: Studies in Philosophical Aesthetics*, edited by Eva Schaper (Cambridge: Cambridge University Press, 1983). This piece was subsequently reprinted, in edited versions, in *Aesthetics: A Reader in Philosophy of the Arts*, edited by D. Goldblatt and L. Brown (Upper Saddle River, New Jersey: Prentice-Hall, 1997), and in *Aesthetics: An Oxford Reader*, edited by P. Maynard and S. Feagin (Oxford and New York: Oxford University Press, 1997). A few years before those reprintings it was published, curiously, in Finnish translation in *Kauneudesta kauhuun taide ja filosofia* 2, edited by Arto Haapala and Markus Lammenranta (Helsinki, 1993), where it is called "*Vitsi.*" I am unable to read any Finnish whatever, and I have been puzzled by the appearance in the Finnish translation of footnotes that are not in the original English. It is my guess and fear that those footnotes are explanations of the jokes in the essay.

my joke is a working knowledge of the English language. But you may need a good bit more, as the background information becomes ever more specific and arcane. Some of the most strongly conditional hermetic jokes are ones involving the topics and jargon of a profession. Some such jokes are not actually *within* the profession. For instance, this doctor joke:

Four doctors went duck hunting together. Together in the duck blind, they decided that instead of all shooting away at the same time, they would take turns as each duck came by. The first to have a shot would be the general practitioner, next would be the internist, then the surgeon, and finally the pathologist.

When the first bird flew over, the general practitioner lifted his shotgun, but never fired, saying, "I'm not sure that was a duck."

The second bird was the internist's. He aimed and followed the bird in his sights, saying, "It looks like a duck, it flies like a duck, it sounds like a duck . . . ," but then the bird was out of range and the internist didn't take a shot.

As soon as the third bird appeared, flying up out of the water only a few feet from the blind, the surgeon blasted away, emptying his pump gun and blowing the bird to smithereens. Turning to the pathologist, the surgeon said, "Go see whether that was a duck."

Or this mathematician joke:

To tell a mathematician from a physicist, it is enough to administer this test. Send the person into a cabin in the woods, telling him his problem is to boil water. If you have previously put a pot in the cabin, and arranged for the stove to be hooked up and for there to be a working sink, then both a mathematician and a physicist will proceed to run water into the pot, put the pot on the stove, turn on the gas, and bring the water to a boil. You cannot tell them apart. But if you fill the pot with water beforehand, then you can tell. The physicist will carry the pot to the stove, turn on the gas, and bring the water to a boil. The mathematician will empty the pot in the sink, thereby reducing this to the first problem, which has already been solved.

Or this philosopher joke:

The president of a small college desires to improve his school's academic reputation. He is told that the best way to do this is to create at least a few first-rank departments. It would be good to work on the mathematics department, he is told, because that would not be too expensive. Mathematicians do not require laboratories or even much equipment. All they need are pencils, paper, and wastebaskets. It might be even better to work on the philosophy department. The philosophers don't need wastebaskets.

You need not be a doctor or a mathematician or a philosopher to appreciate these jokes, nor even know much at all about doctoring, mathematics, or philosophy. At most you need some acquaintance with the presumed proclivity of surgeons to cut first and then diagnose, of mathematicians' curious notions of elegance, and of philosophers' professional license to say anything they want because there is no way to prove them wrong, and so they are permitted to do anything they can get away with (like writing a book about jokes).[8] These three jokes do require something specific of their audiences, but they are only mildly hermetic. A slightly more intricate example is this:

Early one morning a man awoke in a state of terrible anxiety because of the dream he had been having. He immediately called his psychiatrist, and after making

8. But surely it is not only philosophers, and among philosophers it is not only Hegel, about whom it might be said, "He never had a thought he didn't publish."

> a special plea because of his distress he was granted
> an appointment that morning even though it was not
> the day for seeing his psychiatrist. When he arrived in
> the doctor's office, he said, "I had the most awful
> dream you can imagine. In it I raped my mother,
> killed my wife, and seduced my daughter, and more
> things worse than those. I woke up shaking and sweat-
> ing, and I called you immediately. Then I had a quick
> piece of toast and some coffee, and ran down here to
> see you."
>
> "What?" said the psychiatrist. "You call that a
> breakfast?"[9]

For this, one needs to know only two things, although one
other thing deepens the joke. One needs to know the exceptionally high proportion of Jews among psychiatrists, and
to know the commonplace about Jewish mothers that they
are excessively concerned, especially about food. The joke is
deeper for those who believe it an occupational hazard of psy-
chiatry that its practitioners tend to look for deep and convo-
luted explanations when simple and direct ones would do,
and, conversely, that they tend to look only at the surface in
the few cases in which something hidden is at work.

Strongly hermetic jokes require audiences with at least
some substantive knowledge of their topics, and such jokes do
not always require the information and jargon of professions,
but only some significant acquaintance with a specific subject,
like this one, for which you need to know a little about drama:

> A panhandler approached a man on the street outside
> a theater. The man declined to give anything, saying,
> "'Neither a borrower nor a lender be.'—William
> Shakespeare."
>
> The panhandler replied, "'Fuck you!'—David
> Mamet."

9. David Malament, who has taught me many, many things, taught me
this joke.

This one needs an audience with at least some knowledge of the history of formal logic:

What did Lesniewski say to Lukasiewicz?
"Logically, we're poles apart."[10]

Here is one only for those who know a common Yiddish word (which is not so improbable) and also a particularly arcane topic set by Nelson Goodman in the theory of induction:

What is a goy?
A goy is a person who is a girl if examined at any
time up to and including t, and a boy if examined at
any time after t.[11]

And this one needs hearers who know at least a little of problems of reference in the philosophy of language, along with some slight information about ancient Greek literature:

One day a paleographer came into his classics depart-
ment in great excitement. "There has been an earth-
shaking discovery," he announced. "The *Iliad* and the
***Odyssey* were not written by Homer, but by some**
other Greek with the same name."

For jokes that are severely hermetic, deeply embedded in particular cultures, one finds some of the best and worst examples among mathematician jokes.

What's round and purple, and commutes to work?
An Abelian grape.

---

10. This classical composition is by Michael Slote.
11. When I first published this joke, I attributed it to my friend George Boolos, who later told me the joke had been created by Richard Jeffrey, who in turn told me it had been created by Sidney Morgenbesser. I recounted all this in a subsequent correction of the original publication, and sent the whole thing to Boolos. It was a great pleasure to me to know that Boolos had kept the correction posted in his office at M.I.T. When George Boolos died not long ago, we lost a fine friend, a very good philosopher, a man devoted to scholarly exactitude, and one hell of a good man to exchange jokes with.

The audience for this joke first needs some acquaintance with grape jokes, and then it needs to know, at least roughly, what commutativity is, and what an Abelian group is. (I suppose the audience needn't already know that Abelian groups are commutative, but it is unlikely that it would know all the rest and not know that.) Sometimes the condition required is not especially arcane, but it is relatively complex.

> **According to Freud, what comes between fear and sex?**
> *Fünf.*

Here one needs to know that Freud's language was German, that Freud wrote about things like fear and sex (and, of course, one has to understand 'fear' and 'sex' in English), and how to count up to six in German.

With some hermetic jokes what is required is not knowledge, or belief, in the first instance, but an awareness of what might be called "commonplaces."

> **A young Catholic woman told her friend, "I told my husband to buy all the Viagra he can find."**
> **Her Jewish friend replied, "I told my husband to buy all the stock in Pfizer he can find."**

It is not required that the audience (or the teller) actually *believe* that Jewish women are more interested in money than in sex, but he must be acquainted with this idea. When jokes play upon commonplaces—which may or may not be believed—they often do it by exaggeration. Typical examples are clergymen jokes. For instance,

> **After knowing one another for a long time, three clergymen—one Catholic, one Jewish, and one Episcopalian—have become good friends. When they are together one day, the Catholic priest is in a sober, reflective mood, and he says, "I'd like to confess to you that although I have done my best to keep my faith, I have occasionally lapsed, and even since my**

seminary days I have, not often, but sometimes, suc-
cumbed and sought carnal knowledge."

"Ah well," says the rabbi, "it is good to admit these
things, and so I will tell you that, not often, but sometimes, I break the dietary laws and eat forbidden
food."

At this the Episcopalian priest, his face reddening,
says, "If only I had so little to be ashamed of. You
know, only last week I caught myself eating a main
course with my salad fork."

I do not know exactly where jokes come from (nor does
anyone else), but it is my sense that clergymen jokes have often originated in New England, and whether or not that is true,
it is almost certain that the earlier versions are of the interfaith
variety just exemplified, and that the form was later adapted
for intrafaith purposes, as in,

Three rabbis, one Orthodox, one Conservative, and
one Reform, are accustomed to playing golf together
every Sunday. On one particular Sunday their play is
going very slowly because the foursome ahead of
them is playing very slowly. In annoyance, the rabbis
send one of their caddies ahead to speed things up, to
tell the foursome ahead to play faster or to let the rabbis play through.

When the caddie returns he looks crestfallen, and
he says, "I am so ashamed. The foursome ahead is
playing slowly because all four of them are blind.
Blind golfers have to play slowly. They must wait
while their caddies find their balls and then align
them to swing in the right direction. And there I was,
complaining. As soon as I learned, I was so embarrassed. I apologized and left."

"Oh my," says the Orthodox rabbi. "I am humiliated."

"Me too," says the Conservative rabbi. "I think we
should pray for those less fortunate and remind our-

selves, as the Torah says, not to put obstacles in the path of the blind."

"Right," says the Reform rabbi. "Yeah, fine. Why the hell don't they play at night?"

Jokes like these, besides being caustic and possibly unflattering, sometimes incorporate genuine profundity. For instance,

After many days of hard, continuous rain, the river is in danger of flooding, and word goes out that people may have to abandon their homes. When the river crests, water pours through the town, inundating houses, and it continues to rise. Firemen are sent in a small motorboat to go through the streets to make sure everyone is leaving. When they come to the house of the rabbi, they find him standing knee-deep in water on his front porch.

"Come on, Rabbi," say the firemen. "The river will go much higher, and you should leave with us."

"No," says the rabbi. "God will protect me." And he sends them away.

The river rises higher, the rabbi is forced to go up to the second floor of his house, and now the police come in a motor launch.

"Come on, Rabbi," say the police, "there isn't much time."

"No," insists the rabbi. "I will stay right here. God will look after me." And he sends them away.

Now the river rises so high that the rabbi is forced to stand on the roof of his house. When the National Guard arrive in a large boat, telling him that the river is sure to go even higher, the rabbi says, "All my life I have been a man of faith, and I will stay now, and trust in God," and sends them away.

The river rises, the rabbi is swept away, and the rabbi drowns.

Forthwith the rabbi appears in heaven, where he an-

grily approaches the throne of God, demanding, "How
can You have let this happen to me? For all my life I
have kept Your *mitzvot*. I have done what You asked,
and trusted in You. Why?"

A voice sounds from the throne: "You shmuck. I
sent three boats."

I suppose some hearers might find these jokes unflattering,
but I doubt that the jokes are found very offensive. I doubt that
New Yorkers or citizens of New Jersey object to either of these:

A family from Nebraska went to New York City for
the first time on a week's vacation. After being bat-
tered by New York and its citizens for the first few
days, the entire family felt exhausted and humiliated,
and they were nearly ready to cut their vacation short,
but the father insisted on trying once more to have an
agreeable vacation in New York. The family walked
out of their hotel in the morning, and the father went
up to a traffic policeman and inquired, "Officer, would
you tell me the way to the United Nations building, or
should I just go fuck myself?"[12]

How is the alphabet recited in New Jersey?
"Fuckin' A, fuckin' B, fuckin' C. . . ."[13]

It is difficult to say just when such jokes become genuinely
offensive. What do you make of this one?

12. My friend the learned and talented Nicholas Rudall tells this joke in a
version in which a Pakistani approaches a bowler-wearing gentleman on the
streets of London. I do not think either version is superior, but the New York
version tends to work in both England and the United States, while the London
version does not always succeed in the United States. There is no doubt, however, that Mr. Rudall tells his version far better than I tell mine: he does the
Pakistani far better than I do the Nebraskan.

13. A few years ago the distinguished Chicago architect Michael Rosen
supervised the construction of an office building he designed in New Jersey.
Mr. Rosen tells me that this may not be a joke.

What does it say on the bottom of a Polish Coke
bottle?
   Open other end.

Understanding this joke certainly does not require believing
that Poles are stupid or inept. It requires understanding something like "what a Polish joke is." This is not a difficult understanding, and it isn't essentially different from what is required
to understand Irish jokes (made in England), Ukrainian jokes
(made in Russia), Russian jokes (made in Poland), Newfie
jokes (made in Canada), Sikh jokes (made in India), Iowa legislator and Texas Aggie jokes (made in the good old U.S.A.,
along with Polish jokes). And yet these jokes are not equally
appreciated, however well they are understood. All things being equal, a joke in which a rabbi makes an ass of a priest is
likelier to succeed with a Jewish audience than with a Catholic
one, although the joke is completely understood on all sides.
This is due to another kind of condition.

Conditional jokes that depend upon feelings in the audience, likes and dislikes, and preferences, I call *affective*. Typically, these jokes are understood by many people, but the success of the jokes—their capacity to amuse—depends upon the
affective disposition of the audience. It isn't always simply a
matter of succeeding, or not, but a question of degree of success. For instance,

**The thing about German food is that no matter how
much you eat, an hour later you're hungry for power.**

This joke is largely unavailable to anyone who doesn't know
the old chestnut about Chinese food invariably leaving one
hungry soon after eating, whether one believes that about Chinese food or not. But then one must also know the commonplace about Germans that they long to control others, to have
and to wield power. Now it makes some difference whether
one only knows this commonplace, or whether one knows it
and believes it to be true. And finally, it matters whether one
has negative feelings about Germans on that count, or doesn't.

If it offends one to have Germans represented in this way, then the amusement may be lost altogether.

It is not only affective jokes that can have this variable success. With hermetic jokes, as well, there may be levels of response depending upon just how much the audience can bring to the joke. For instance,

> Not long after the Six-Day War in the Middle East, a class was meeting in the Soviet Union, a class in the Russian War College. The problem under discussion that day was how the Soviet Union might fight a war against China. Some of the students were distressed and puzzled, and one of them said, "How could we possibly fight a war against China? We could put at most, what, 150 or 200 million soldiers in the field? The enemy would have an army of nearly a billion. It would be hopeless."
>
> "Not necessarily," said the teacher, a distinguished Soviet Army commander. "It is entirely possible for the smaller army to win. Just notice what happened not long ago in the Middle East. Israel can field an army of at most 2 or 3 million soldiers, while the combined Arab armies number 100 million, and yet Israel won that war."
>
> "Yes," objected the student, "but where can we find 3 million Jews?"[14]

Beneath the twist in this story, the idea that the Soviet officer-candidate did not see how to transfer the lesson of Israel to the Soviet Union, is the savage irony of the fact that at the time of the Six-Day War there were far more than 3 million Jews in the Soviet Union, many of them there only because they were not permitted to emigrate.

Here is another multilayered hermetic joke, this one less bitter:

---

14. I owe this to Amos Cohen, who not only told me the joke but also pointed out its bitter aftertaste. He credits the joke to Rabbi Elliot Gertel.

A musician was performing a solo recital in Israel.
When he ended the last selection, a thunderous response came from the audience, including many cries
of "Play it again." He stepped forward, bowed, and
said, "What a wonderfully moving response. Of
course I shall be delighted to play it again." And he
did. At the end, again there was a roar from the audience, and again many cries of "Play it again." This
time the soloist came forward smiling and said,
"Thank you. I have never been so touched in all my
concert career. I should love to play it again, but there
is no time, for I must perform tonight in Tel Aviv. So,
thank you from the bottom of my heart—and fare-
well." Immediately a voice was heard from the back of
the hall saying, "You will stay here and play it again
until you get it right."

This is a pretty good joke just as it stands, with no background conditions beyond some obvious knowledge of what
music recitals are like, and in this respect it is one of those
"Jewish" jokes that needn't be told or heard by Jews in order
to succeed. But something is added for those who know of the
extremely confident music audience to be found in Israel, especially the very sophisticated, self-applauding German Jews.
And then there is more. The total riches of this joke are available only to those who know the Jewish religious requirement
that on certain occasions the appropriate portion of the Hebrew Bible be read out, that those present make known any
errors they detect in the reading, and that the reader not only
acknowledge these corrections but that he then go back and
read out the text correctly, and that he stay there and read it
again until he gets it right. It is this last piece of information
that makes for yet another level in the joke, and, so I think,
makes it a better joke than the version I have often heard in
which the performer is a tenor singing arias in Italy. In Italy,
too, there is the presumption of a supremely confident audience, especially for singing, which is why it should be not a

pianist but a tenor, but it is not there that there is the connection with a required public performance ordained on religious-legal grounds. Here is another salient point of comparison of jokes with works of art. Shakespeare's *Hamlet* certainly is accessible to those who know only one meaning of the word 'nunnery,' but for those who know that in Shakespeare's time the word was slang for a brothel, there is more in the play when Hamlet says to Ophelia, "Get thee to a nunnery."

If all jokes are conditional, at least to some degree, then what difference does it make that they call for a contribution from the audience? And why can't the joke-teller simply inform his audience in advance, tell them whatever they need to know in order to get his joke? Or, why can't the audience accept the joke conditionally?

Suppose you tell me that Noah Cohen could not now become president of the United States. I don't believe you. You tell me that he is only eighteen years old, and that one must be at least thirty-five years old to be president according to the United States Constitution. Suppose I don't know how old Noah Cohen is, and I don't know this constitutional provision. If I believe you about those things, then I will believe that he can't become president. But even if I don't believe you, I certainly can believe this: If a person must be at least thirty-five years old to be president, and if Noah Cohen is eighteen years old, then Noah Cohen could not now become president of the United States. That is, I can certainly believe the conditional statement without believing the if-parts. Can I do something like this with a joke?

Suppose I am not a mathematician, and I don't know about grape jokes, and so in order to tell me about the Abelian grape, you first tell me what I need to know. Grape jokes are like elephant jokes, you explain, those jokes in which the word 'elephant' is in the answer to a question.

What's big and gray, and wrote gloomy poetry?
T. S. Elephant.

What's big and gray, and sang both jazz and popular
songs?
   Elephants Gerald.[15]

Grape jokes are like that, except that the word 'grape' is in
the answer to a question. Like

What's round and purple, and conquered the world?
Alexander the Grape.

Then you go on to teach me, superficially, enough elementary mathematics: I learn a little about sets, about groups, and
about the relations of members of sets and groups one to another, including the relations of associativity and commutativity. And then you give me the Abelian grape joke. Will this
work? Will I now realize that if mathematical groups are like
that, and there is this institution of grape jokes, then your joke
is funny? Will I find the joke funny? Highly unlikely, but exactly why is this enterprise so misguided?

The first thing to note is that, so encumbered, the joke
seems labored, and even contrived. Good jokes, and perhaps
jokes in general, tend to be concise (which is not to deny that
there are wonderful jokes of great length; "Berl-in-debate-with-
the-priest" is an example—see the appendix), and why is that?
It may be that jokes are most appreciated when they are brisk
and not weighed down, but I think it is a mistake to think
that it is the concision itself that matters. What matters is what
makes the concision possible. What makes it possible is that
so much can go unsaid. And why can it go unsaid? *Because the*
audience already knows it.

It is a general thesis of mine that a deep satisfaction in successful joke transactions is the sense held mutually by teller
and hearer that they are joined in feeling. As I noted earlier,
jokes do not *compel* a sequel, not in the way, say, that argu-

15. Although some jokes are virtually impossible to write, like the Freud-
fear-sex joke, some seem to me even more effective when written. This one,
about Elephants Gerald (Ella Fitzgerald), works even better when seen.

ments do. Not only is the effect not forced on the audience, but there is nothing especially acute to say when one's joke fails. When one's argument fails to move someone, when it fails to elicit a belief, one may always write this off to the benighted condition of the audience. They have been unable to follow the argument, or they are too ignorant to accept the premises, perhaps. But with a joke that has gone flat, all the teller is entitled to suppose is that his audience doesn't share his sense of humor. He may be bold enough, and confident enough in his fine joke, as well as in his ability to tell it, to go so far as to deny that his audience has any sense of humor whatever. But he cannot *prove* that, not in the way in which one might prove that one's argument is valid, and thereby consign the unmoved audience to the ranks of the irrational, the inattentive, or the downright stupid. All you can say of the fellow who doesn't laugh at your joke, at least all you can say when it has been established that he understands you, that he gets the joke, is that *he is not like you,* at least not in regard to the dynamics of your joke. And even if the joke has worked with everyone else, even if gets a good laugh from everyone else you or anyone else has tried it on, still this unlaughing listener is, in the end, nothing worse than not like you. He is not less human, at least not in any demonstrable regard. He is like someone who isn't enraptured by Mozart's *Marriage of Figaro,* who doesn't swoon at a fabulous Rembrandt, or who doesn't care to turn his head to see the sun set behind a mountain, or to see the colors of the ocean change as the sun plays upon the water.

How important is that? Surely you can inhabit a world with this person, even though he is a kind of stranger to you. Later I will urge you to agree that this estrangement is very important indeed, and that it can represent a threat to one's conception of his own humanity, and I will be insisting that this infirmity shows in failed jokes just as surely as in failures to care for the same art, but until then I want only to note that what has failed is the effort to achieve an intimacy between teller and hearer. It is a failure to join one another in a community of appreciation. It is exactly this community that begins to be marshaled

when conditional jokes are told. These are the jokes that require the audience to supply something, and it is essential in
the effect of such jokes that the audience be allowed to supply
this. In fact they are urged to supply it, virtually compelled to
supply it automatically, without even considering whether they
would like to be thus pulled in. You cannot do this to someone,
you cannot capture him by playing on what he knows and
feels, if you first have to instruct him. Instructing him leaves
him passive; it does not pull him toward you in terms of what
you already share, precisely because you do not already share
it. Consider this joke, which is available to both Jews and non-
Jews, but has a greater or a different kick for Jews:

> Abe and his friend Sol are out for a walk together in a
> part of town they haven't been in. Passing a Christian
> church, they notice a curious sign in front saying
> "$1,000 to anyone who will convert." "I wonder what
> that's about," says Abe. "I think I'll go in and have a
> look. I'll be back in a minute; just wait for me."
>
> Sol sits on a sidewalk bench and waits patiently for
> nearly half an hour, and then Abe reappears.
>
> "Well," asks Sol, "what are they up to? Who are
> they trying to convert? Why do they care? Did you get
> the $1,000?"
>
> Indignantly, Abe replies, "Money. That's all you
> people care about."

Think of trying to tell this joke to someone who is not only
ignorant of the widespread idea that Jews care more about
money than almost anything else, but also does not even recognize 'Abe' and 'Sol' as Jewish names. Of course you could begin
by telling him about those names, and then go on to inform
him of this idea about Jews, and you might do this at considerable length, mentioning the character of Shylock, mistaken
histories of the practice of usury during the Middle Ages, and
whatever else you think will fortify a rich sense of the idea. Do
you think the joke will work then?

Certainly it won't work well, if at all. Why not? Because you need your audience to know something *in advance of the joke,* and you need them to know it without your telling them. In this respect it is not like the solution to a puzzle or a mathematical problem. Suppose the problem is how to ensure that a pie will be cut into six equal slices, when the pie is to be sliced by one of those who will be given a slice. The solution, assuming the rationality of the man with the knife, and assuming that he is skilled enough to cut a slice that will be any reasonable fraction of the whole pie, is to stipulate that after each slice has been cut, all those except the slicer will be given the opportunity to select the just-sliced piece. Thus the only way for the person cutting the pie to ensure that he will have a piece no smaller than one-sixth of the pie is to cut the pie into six equal pieces.

It is perfectly possible to give this solution to someone, and to have it fully appreciated by the recipient, even if he has no advance knowledge of the problem. You might simply explain the problem to him, and then offer the solution. You cannot do this with a joke, at least not without considerable cost to the joke-transaction, and the reason is that you need to begin with an implicit acknowledgment of a shared background, a background of awareness that you both are already in possession of and bring to the joke. This is the foundation of the intimacy that will develop if your joke succeeds, and the hearer then also joins you in a shared response to the joke.

And just what is this *intimacy*? It is the shared sense of those in a *community*. The members know that they are in this community, and they know that they are joined there by one another. When the community is focused on a joke, the intimacy has two constituents. The first constituent is a shared set of beliefs, dispositions, prejudices, preferences, et cetera—a shared outlook on the world, or at least part of an outlook. The second constituent is a shared feeling—a shared response to something. The first constituent can be cultivated and realized without jokes. So can the second constituent, but with jokes, the second constituent is amplified by the first, and this is a very curious and wonderful fact about jokes.

I may overvalue the intimacy available through joke-telling; after all, I am one of those who love and need joke-telling. But I am confident that it is an intimacy that should not be underestimated. When we laugh at the same thing, that is a very special occasion. It is already noteworthy that we laugh at all, at anything, and that we laugh all alone. That we do it *together* is the satisfaction of a deep human longing, the realization of a desperate hope. It is the hope that we are enough like one another to sense one another, to be able to live together.

When you have good reasons for believing something, you expect me to join you in your belief once you have given me your reasons. And if I fail, you may be troubled by my failure, but you will indeed consider it a *failure,* and you will consign me to the ranks of the cognitively defective. When you find a joke funny, you expect me to join you in your amusement once you have told me the joke. If I fail, then once you have determined that I understand the joke, exactly what *failure* will you attribute to me? You find the joke funny, I don't. It is not as if some argument or proof had been presented, with your following to the conclusion and my not. In that case, the conclusion is something *to be believed.* This is an objective matter. My failure to join you is an error, or a mistake, or a misapprehension. But with the unsuccessful joke, there is nothing to point to besides the joke itself. You cannot show that the joke is an instance of something that must be acknowledged as funny, as you might show that an argument is an instance of valid reasoning. So you point to the joke. In fact, you tell it. Why do you expect me to find it funny? And just what is it you want of me, in wanting me to find it funny? What is it you want beyond the satisfaction you get from succeeding—and succeeding at what?

I think what you want is to *reach* me, and therein to verify that you understand me, at least a little, which is to exhibit that we are, at least a little, alike. This is the establishment of a felt intimacy between us.

I have been making heavy weather of this *intimacy,* as I am calling it, this community of amusement we belong to when we are laughing at the same joke, and I had better say something about why it seems to me such an important human achievement, virtually indispensable despite being something no one can guarantee—indeed *because* it cannot be guaranteed.

There are two ways in which you and I might agree. We might both believe the same thing, perhaps for just the same reasons. And we might feel the same way about something. In the first case, say, we both believe that the coast of Maine in the summer is characteristically a warm but not hot place, with a rockbound shoreline, often with mountains nearby, and near the coast there is often a persistent fog. In the second case, we find Maine in the summer rather melancholy, with beauty no doubt, but a beauty that seems dim and fragile, and we feel sweetly blue to be there.

The climatology of Maine is an objective fact. I have learned it firsthand, and if you have not yet learned it that way, you can look it up, or you can listen to me and believe me, or you might sojourn up there to check it out for yourself. In the end, if you do not agree with me, I will have to suppose that you don't know how to observe, or you didn't check the right references, or you haven't adequate eyesight, or something else keeps you from latching on to the objective features of the world, or at least of Maine.

The *feel* of Maine in the summer, however, is another matter. If you don't feel about Maine as I do, then you may yet "understand" my semi-sadness at being there by grasping my best descriptions of myself-in-Maine. (It is one of the great achievements of art to provide for this kind of communication.) But even if you have a thorough grasp of my state, you still do not agree with me *in feeling*. You do not have the feeling yourself. I am alone with my feeling, at least so far as you are concerned, and you and I are not in communion in this matter. So what? Well, let us try thinking of this with reference to a joke. Take this gem:

What do Alexander the Great and Winnie the Pooh have in common?
They have the same middle name.

I can say something about why that tickles me, how it calls up the question of just what a name is, and the memory of what a child takes himself to be doing when he learns some-one's name, and Milne's cleverness in building a kind of name on the model of historical nomenclature, and things like that. And I'm sure you can follow that. But what if you are not amused by the joke? The thing amuses me and it doesn't amuse you, and that's that. Yes, but why is that that? It is because (and now you must indulge me) there is something in me that is reached by this joke, and this something is not in you. This doesn't mean you are deficient, that I am somehow more than you, any more than it would mean that if I had an ingrown toenail and you didn't. But it does mean that you are not *like* me, at least not in this inner something that is tickled by the idea of Winnie the Pooh's middle name. And why does that matter to me?

Why do we recommend these things to one another, any-way? Why point out the huge, bright new moon, the funny stuff happening on *King of the Hill* on television (calling me into the room to watch it with you), the gritty beauty of the waterfront in Gdansk? Why draw one another's attention to all that stuff? Because we wish one another well? Well, maybe, but at its core I do not think this is entirely a matter of altruism. I think it is a wish, a need, a longing to *share* these things, to feel them together. And it is not quite enough to explain this to say that we are, after all, communal creatures, although I suppose we are. The other component in the explanation is the fact that I need reassurance that this something inside me, the something that is tickled by a joke, is indeed something that constitutes an element of my humanity. I discover something of what it is to be a human being by finding this thing in me, and then having it echoed in you, another human being.

Of course I want you to like the one about Winnie the Pooh. I want you to like it because I like you and I want you to have something you like, and I want you to be grateful to me for supplying it. But I also need you to like it, because in your liking I receive a confirmation of my own liking. I put this by saying that the joke *is funny,* as if this were an objective matter, like there being damned little sand along the coast of Maine, but what I mean is that I laugh at it, and if everyone laughed at it, then it would really *be* funny (or as good as funny), and I do so want you to laugh at it.

It is one thing to worry over a version of eighteenth-century skepticism, and wonder whether green looks green to you the way it does to me, and what it would mean to inhabit a world in which we did not experience green the same way, and what it means that we seemingly do inhabit a world in which we can't be "sure" that we see green together. It is quite another thing to wonder what the world would be like for me if I never found the same things funny that you or anyone else find funny. I personally have no worries on account of the problem about green, but I worry and feel stricken every time one of my jokes does not reach you.

3

WHEN JOKES ARE ASYMMETRICAL

I HAVE BEEN SPEAKING AS IF, in the purveyance of a conditional joke, both the teller and the audience satisfy the condition, and I suppose this is the central, normal case, and indeed it is the model for the kind of intimacy I have been extolling, but the case can be otherwise. If the joke is hermetic or affective, there are particular beliefs or feelings presumed by the joke, and it is possible for either the teller or the audience not to meet the presumption. When the teller and his audience do not share the relevant background, let me call the joke-telling *asymmetrical*. A common, and I think disgusting, example occurs when some adult urges a child to tell a joke the child does not understand, thinking it somehow cute that the child tell a good joke without understanding it. But there are more complex and interesting examples of failures of teller and hearer both to satisfy a joke's conditions. It is possible for a joke to be so ineptly located that it has no chance, even ceases to be a joke. This joke is like that:

> What goes "Ho de do, ho de do?"
> A couple of black guys running for the elevator.

In the rural South, this joke makes no sense, for the allegedly parodied speech is no more typical of black men than of anyone else. For the joke to have a chance, it must be told against a background in which black men talk like that but white men don't, and it needs an audience itself located in that background.

Think of an anti-Semitic joke, or an anti-black joke. Now imagine the joke told in every combination of circumstances— a Jew tells it to Jews, a Jew tells it to non-Jews, a non-Jew tells it to Jews, a non-Jew tells it to non-Jews. Not only will the joke work differently (if it works at all) in different circumstances, but it may also, so to speak, change its "meaning."

It is not always known in advance who satisfies the conditions. Indeed, one way of discovering whether or not you and others have certain things in common is to tell them a conditional joke, and then learn whether your audience satisfies the condition by noting whether and how they take your joke. Try this one on various audiences:

> An American tourist in Brazil was sitting on the beach when he noticed two older men sitting together talking. To his amazement they looked just like Hitler and Goebbels, and so he listened in on their conversation.
> "We came close," said the Hitler look-alike, "and next time, soon, we will succeed."
> "Yes," said the other, "and this time we will finish off all the Jews and the electricians."
> At this the tourist could not help interrupting, and he said, "Why the electricians?"
> "You see?" said the Goebbels-looking man. "I told you no one would care about the Jews."

This joke will work with just about anyone, even those who do not think of Brazil as a haven for Nazis, but it works differently for those who believe that the world does not care much for Jews, and for those who believe that Jews believe that the world does not care much for Jews.

Sometimes the very elementary understanding of a joke depends upon opinions held by the audience, rather than any particularly arcane material. Here is an exceptionally problematic quip:

Wagner is the Puccini of music.[16]

I once thought of using this example in my work on the logic of metaphor, but I have since discovered that the line simply does not work uniformly well with everyone, and with some listeners it does not work at all. The line is meant to express an exceedingly low opinion of the music of both Wagner and Puccini, and especially of Puccini, and I once thought that it could succeed in doing this regardless of the opinions held by either the teller of the line or any hearer. But if you tell this joke to someone who has a pretty good opinion of both Wagner and Puccini, he is likely to be puzzled. He is not puzzled because metaphors are understandable only to those who agree with them. For instance, you can understand Diana Vreeland's "Pink is the navy blue of India"[17] without agreeing with it: you can *understand* it without knowing whether it is apt. But someone who likes both Wagner and Puccini may have trouble telling what you're driving at when you give him "Wagner is the Puccini of music." He recognizes the form of the quip, *a* is to *b* as *c* is to *d,* but he cannot find the *d.* In "Michael Jordan is the Mozart of basketball," plainly, Jordan is to basketball as Mozart is to music. But here we have Wagner is to music as Puccini is to . . . what? Of course the idea is that Puccini is so bad that what he did doesn't even

16. I heard this example when Jerrold Levinson stunned his audience with it during a lecture at the University of Copenhagen in 1998.
17. I owe this marvelous example to Andy Austin Cohen, who also told me the quip is from Diana Vreeland.

count as music, and whatever it is that he did, he was bad at it. Hence Wagner is bad at music just as Puccini is bad at whatever that is. If you offer this line to someone who has a good opinion of both Wagner and Puccini, he may be unable to figure out what you are driving at, although it is possible for someone who disagrees with you about these composers to pick up your opinion from this line.

All that is at stake in that line about Wagner and Puccini, if anything, is one's opinion of some music, but asymmetrical joke-telling has a place in much more serious investigations. When you induce what is thought to be fellow-feeling by telling a joke, and you yourself do not have the feeling, that is, you do not yourself satisfy the requisite condition, then you are engaged in a kind of fraudulence, and as with all kinds of lying, deceit, and fraudulence, you are subject to moral appraisal.

In the central case, then, a genuine intimacy is sought, and in these deviant, asymmetrical cases, an insincere, hollow intimacy is attempted. For either case we may ask, how is an occasion created for attempting this intimacy?

4

PROBLEMS AND OCCASIONS
FOR JOKE-MAKING

IF THE CREATION OF A JOKE is like the solution of a problem, then how is the problem set? One may simply set a problem for oneself, taking any subject one likes. For instance:

What is Sacramento?
It is the stuffing in a Catholic olive.[18]

---

18. This was made up many years ago, collaboratively, by the remarkable Richard Bernstein and me. No, we don't think it is a great joke. But you try making up something about pimiento.

Or one may be struck by the possibility of playing on certain words, and then undertake to play.

An exhibitionist was thinking of retiring, but he decided to stick it out for one more year.[19]

An eighty-five-year-old says to some of his pals, "You know, I have sex almost every night."
"Really?" asks one of them.
"Yes," replies the man, "for instance this week I had it almost on Monday, almost on Tuesday, almost on Wednesday. . . ."[20]

A man walks into a bar one afternoon, sits on a stool, and asks the bartender for a beer. When the bartender brings the drink he says, "Will you be OK out here for a few minutes? I have to do a few things in back."
"Sure," says the man, "take your time."
Shortly after the bartender leaves for the back room, the man hears someone say, "You're looking pretty good. Have you been working out?"
"Not very much," says the man, as he looks around. But he can see no one. As he turns back to his beer, he hears the voice again: "That's a nice shirt you're wearing. It goes well with your pants."
Again the man can see no one, and he is becoming uneasy when the bartender returns from his errands. He says to the bartender, "The funniest damned thing has been going on. Someone seems to be talking to me, but I can't see anyone."

19. This was relayed to me by Andy Austin Cohen, who got it from her friend Mr. Frank Golonka. Although I have never met him, I have ample evidence that Officer Golonka is an exceptionally accomplished appreciator and teller of jokes. He is also the source of the story on pp. 37–38.
20. Helmut Teichner, an elderly man, told this story as part of a toast he offered to his equally elderly friend who had just been married. Mr. Teichner also told the joke about lawn-mowing (see p. 49), and he told it at a meeting of the Anti-Defamation League after I had delivered a lecture on ethnic humor. Mr. Teichner has a striking knack for finding curiously appropriate jokes for the occasion.

"Oh, that," says the bartender. "It's the peanuts. They're complimentary."[21]

For his eighty-fifth birthday a man's friends decided to give him a visit from an expensive, high-class call girl. The evening of his birthday, she appeared at his door, and when he opened the door she said, "Happy birthday! Your friends have sent you a gift. I'm here to bring you super sex."

The man thought for a moment, and then he said, "At my age, I think I'll have the soup."

Once a couple had the great misfortune to have born to them a child whose body was incomplete. In fact there was nothing to the unfortunate child but a head. But the couple did not despair, and they devoted themselves to rearing their bodiless child, and indeed they succeeded. Year after year they took care of the child and its special needs, until finally its twenty-first birthday arrived. To celebrate they took the child-head with them to their customary neighborhood bar, where they placed the head on the bar between them, and then the husband said, "Today my son is twenty-one years old, and we're celebrating. Drinks for everyone."

When the bartender had served everyone in the room, and everyone had sung "Happy birthday," the mother carefully poured her son's drink into his mouth, and then, to everyone's astonishment, suddenly the boy began to grow, and in a minute he had developed a full torso, complete with arms and hands.

"It's wonderful," exclaimed the boy. "Mother, father, look at me. I have arms and hands. Now I will buy a round of drinks, to celebrate this great development."

The bartender served everyone again. This time the

21. This wonderful, obvious, gentle story is from John Kussmann.

boy said "Look, everyone, now I can handle my own
drink," and he lifted his glass and poured its contents
into his mouth. At that, he began to grow again, and
this time legs and feet appeared, and now he was a
fully normal young man. As soon as his new feet
could touch the floor, he was off the barstool, singing
and prancing about the room, and saying he would
buy another round of drinks. But before the next
round could be served, the young man staggered and
fell to the floor, dead.

Looking across the bar mournfully, the bartender
observed, "He should have quit while he was a head."[22]

But all those cases are somewhat special, and the problem
that inspires joke-creation often comes simply from one's sense
of what people currently are thinking about, or at least are immediately aware of. You can make up a joke about Bill Clinton's
sex life, or Dan Quayle's ignorance. You could make up a joke
about the sex life of any adventurer you know, or about the
misstatements of anyone prone to such remarks. But you cannot assume that any audience will be aware of those people,
and you *can* assume a ready acquaintance with Bill Clinton's
alleged dalliances and Dan Quayle's misspelling. (Of course you
can make up your jokes about those more anonymous figures,
but you will have to tell those jokes to people you know are
aware of these miscreant friends of yours.)

From time to time someone succeeds in introducing a subject for joking that has nothing to do with what's in the news.
It is just a subject that catches the fancy of joke-makers, and it

---

22. I will risk the utterly nonprofessional observation that in jokes incor-
porating plays on words, when the play involves a single word with more than
one meaning (as with the 'complimentary' peanuts), it is easy enough to write
the joke, but when the play is on different words that sound the same (as with
'ahead' / 'a head'), it is impossible to write the joke. My friend Jerrold Sadock,
a distinguished linguist, is at work on a monograph cataloging various kinds
of missed communications. I am flattered that Mr. Sadock has invited me to
illustrate each kind of misfire with a joke, but I must confess that he has forbidden me to attempt the relevant grammatical analyses.

is hard to say why their fancy is caught, although sometimes it is precisely the strangeness and narrowness of the subject that constitutes an irresistible challenge.

It is stimulating to be given a new topos for joking about, and it is even more invigorating when the topic is extremely specific and confined. One is reminded of Stravinsky's observation that the most strict and rigid of musical forms, like the fugue, are the most liberating and inspiring for a composer precisely because they free him from the need to worry about too many possibilities and leave him to exploit his genius by being inventive within given confines. Suppose you are told that there are to be jokes specifically about snails. Here are some examples:

> **What does a snail say when riding on the back of a turtle?**
> "Whee!"

> **A turtle was mugged and robbed by a gang of snails. When the police asked for a description of the villains, the turtle replied, "I'm sorry, but I just don't know. It all happened so fast."**

> **One evening a man hears a faint tapping at his front door. When he opens the door he sees no one, and then he notices a snail on the ground. He picks up the snail and heaves it as far as he can across the lawn. A year later he hears a tapping at the door again, and again when he opens the door nothing is there except the snail, who says, "What the hell was that all about?"**[23]

For an inveterate joke-maker, being given this topic and these examples is like being given the subject for a fugue.

Once some figure or event has taken on sufficient publicity, it becomes almost automatically the core of the "problem." The problem is how to find a play on words, or an imagined

---

23. This delightful subject—the snail joke—was brought to my attention by Bernie Sahlins, who also supplied me with these examples.

congruence of things having to do with Hillary Clinton's health plan, Bill Clinton's trip to China, riots at the World Cup soccer matches, or yet another failure to fly a hot-air balloon around the world. Or, say, how to involve snails in the next Olympics.[24]

If you are a joke-maker, perhaps a creator as well as a retailer, then you know these topics, and you know that your prospective audience knows them. When you offer your joke, you solicit their knowledge, you elicit it, in fact, virtually against their will, and they find themselves contributing the background that will make the joke work. Thus they join you. And then they join you again, if the joke works, in their response, and the two of you find yourselves a community, a community of amusement. This is what I call the *intimacy* of joking.

It is a well-known fact, and for many people a problematic and disturbing fact, that these public topics for joking often and inevitably include misfortunes, sometimes horrible ones. There have been groups of jokes concerning earthquakes, hurricanes, plane crashes, space shuttle disasters, and, above and below all, death. These topics are as suitable as any others for use as public matters about which joke-tellers may assume a common awareness, and thus as occasions for cultivating the intimacy that goes with successful joking; but they have a special urgency all their own. They are topics that are hard to confront, difficult to accept, and yet relentless in their insistence upon our attention. Humor in general and jokes in particular are among the most typical and reliable resources we have for meeting these devastating and incomprehensible matters. No one *understands* death, no one can comprehend it and size it up without remainder, and no one can ignore it.

Many successful jokes incorporate an absurdity, and therein

24. This is a personal communication to Bernie Sahlins, carried out here in public so that those who are able might help us in the project. Bernie, the next Olympics is due in Sydney in 2000. We have until then to work out the details of track and field snails.

lies the lesson that a human response to absurdity is laughter. It is not just jokes, but indeed it is also the world itself and its various inhabitants that are sometimes absurd to human contemplation. When we laugh at a true absurdity, we simultaneously confess that we cannot make sense of it and that we accept it. Thus this laughter is an expression of our humanity, our finite capacity, our ability to live with what we cannot understand or subdue. We can dwell with the incomprehensible without dying from fear or going mad. That may be a religious thought, but I have found it in thinking about the human response to jokes, in the laughter that is absolutely, characteristically, essentially human. And it is doubly so with jokes about death: with them we have the absurdity common to many jokes, and also the incomprehensibility of death itself. I will give you one example:

> Abe visits his doctor for a routine examination and gets the devastating news that he is mortally ill, with no treatment possible, and that he will die within a day. He goes home, tells his wife, Sarah, and after they have absorbed the shock of the terrible news, Abe says to Sarah,
> "Since it is my last night, Sarah, do you think we could go to bed and fool around?"
> "Of course," says Sarah. And so they do.
> Later, at about 1 A.M., Abe wakes up, prods Sarah, and asks, "Do you think we could do it again?"
> "Certainly, Abe, it's your last night." And so they do.
> At 3 A.M. Abe is awake again, and again he asks Sarah for her attentions.
> "For God's sake, Abe, *you* don't have to get up in the morning."

Sarah's remark makes perfect sense, so perfect that it is incredible. The fact of Abe's impending death is impossible to embrace and contemplate, and Sarah's response matches it perfectly.

For very many jokes, we are given a topic, often an esoteric one, and the challenge is to find a joke involving that topic. And for certain kinds of jokes we need some occasion or topic that we can take for granted as part of a shared background with an audience, and we play on that shared background. It is often a help in joke-telling if you can call upon your audience to supply some special information in order to understand the joke. When you do this with your audience, you draw them in, make them part of the whole enterprise.

For the kind of joke that answers a specific, peculiar challenge, we need special audiences, audiences that can understand words in Yiddish or French, or references to things only mathematicians or lawyers or doctors might know, or, as with Robert Pinsky and his late friend Elliot, we need people who know that the problem has been to create a funny story involving two rabbis and the corpse of one Chinese man. The challenge is not always so arcane, and there are plenty of set topics for those who wish to compose solutions. For these jokes, there is a stable of staple topics that continue: Polish jokes, lightbulb-changing jokes, jokes about sex, about Jews, about WASPs, about black people, about Hillary Clinton, et cetera. Among topics always available are those making use of enduring stereotypes, whether or not the stereotypes are believed in. For instance,

A group of Jews decided to take up competitive rowing, and so they formed a crew and began practicing. Months later they had competed several times, and always they not only lost, but came in so far behind that they thought something must be wrong with their approach. They sent one of their number off to England to observe the Oxford/Cambridge race, and then to the Ivy League to see the rowers there. When he returned, he was asked if indeed these other crews had a different technique.

"Well," he reported, "they have *one* guy *yelling,* and *eight* guys *rowing.*"

For a somewhat different kind of joke we need a topic or event that seizes the attention of many people, because these jokes are, so to speak, meant for everyone. For a general audience, we need something that everyone can be expected to know, and for this we need something widely publicized, and anything like this will be an obvious candidate for jokes, no matter how solemn the event or serious the topic. Thus we have jokes about the Polish pope, the illness of Ronald Reagan, the crashes of airplanes, and the blowing-up of a federal building, and also about imagined events, like World War III.

There is no more durable topic than death. It is permanent and universal. Everyone is aware of it; everyone will know what you are talking about the moment you mention death. In this regard, death is like sex (sex may be like death in other regards as well, but that is not our business here), and marriage and illness and love and youth and old age—all things that we can presume many of us know about. Those who know one of these things, know it intimately, at first hand, are apt to make use of jokes not equally available to others. For instance,

One good thing about Alzheimer's disease is that if you get it, you can hide your own Easter eggs.

Some find that joke especially disagreeable, but among those who like it best are some people actually suffering from the disease, and the people who tend them. Illness, love, sex, and the rest are well known to very many of us, but within this group death is the most universal: not everyone grows old or knows older people, not everyone can remember his or her youth, not everyone has the good and bad luck of being in love, not everyone gets married or unmarried, not everyone is sometimes ill—but everyone knows about death. If you wish to tell a joke to the largest possible audience, you need a presumed background shared by everyone, and you cannot do better than to presume that everyone in your audience has thought about death.

When we think of death, why do we think to joke about it? Every general theory of jokes known to me is wrong. Such a monotonic theory always seizes upon one or two kinds of jokes, and misses other kinds. For instance, many people think the main kind of joke is one made by people about those they imagine to be their inferiors, or jokes made by those with power about those who are powerless. And there are many such jokes. But the reverse also happens. Those who are oppressed make jokes about their oppressors. Thus in the 1930s and 1940s Jews made jokes about Germans. All through the career of the Soviet Union, Russians made jokes about Russian communists, and Poles did and still do make jokes about Russians.

When you make a joke about those more powerful than you, and even those who control your life, it is a way of striking back, of taking a kind of control over those people. It is a poor substitute, perhaps, for real power, but it may be all that is available. If your joke works, you will make people laugh at your oppressor, and if you are very lucky (and your joke is very good), you may even make your oppressor laugh at himself.

Now of course the one thing with power over us all is death. To joke about death is a way of domesticating something that essentially cannot be tamed. You can hope for the end of the Soviet Union, for the end of racism, for peace in the Middle East, for the death of a tyrant; and these may be very long shots, but they are *possible*. There is no possibility of escaping death. (Christianity promises one kind of escape from death, but even that promise does not exempt any of us from dying.)

The idea of death can be terrifying, numbing, incomprehensible. Joking about it returns a kind of balance. It is a way of being in charge, even of death. A way of being in charge of something, sometimes, is simply being able to speak about it, because if you can speak about it, it hasn't numbed you completely, hasn't robbed you of everything. In a hospital waiting room I once overheard a doctor telling another doctor that he had just found a way to tell his patient that the patient would die. The first doctor had said to his patient, "Well, you won't have to pay income tax this year." Not a great joke, but not bad, and noteworthy, because doctors, in my experience, do not do so well in the joking business. And noteworthy as well because it is an illustration of the use of joking as a way of restoring to oneself enough power and control to speak of the unspeakable.

These seem to me the answers to two good questions. Why do we take death as a topic for joking? Death is the ultimately public, absolutely common topic. Why do we deal with death by telling jokes? Death is the ultimate oppressor. There is a convergence on this phenomenon: jokes about death are virtually inevitable, and they will be with us until either we stop joking altogether, or we stop dying.

5

JEWISH JOKES AND THE ACCEPTANCE OF ABSURDITY

DEATH IS THE FINAL ABSURDITY, perhaps, but it is not the only one, and death is not the only absurdity jokes can embrace. It is especially noteworthy among the traditions of Jewish joke-telling that jokes can be offered as responses to incomprehensibilities, and there seems to me to be a sanction for this within the traditions of Judaism itself. Of course there are jokes that are recognizably Jewish. And of course one cannot say just what the Jewishness in these jokes is. There are Jewish jokes that seem to have nothing in common with one another, nothing thematic or stylistic. And every Jewish joke has a mate in some joke that seems not really a Jewish joke. And yet there may be something to say about some Jewish jokes if, as I think, their apology is a specifically Jewish sanction for humor. The sanction is biblical, and even Talmudic. The jokes it underwrites may belong to a class that has necessary and sufficient conditions, but I have too much heart to attempt to formulate them. I will characterize them by means of a few examples along the way.

When I first thought of characterizing jokes like these, it seemed right to say that they all display a crazy logic. They have an insane rationality, a logical rigor gone over the edge. For instance, in this:

> A man is lying asleep in bed with his wife one night when she wakes him, saying, "Close the window; it's cold outside."
>
> He grunts, rolls over, and goes back to sleep.
>
> His wife nudges him. "Close the window; it's cold outside."
>
> He moans, pulls the blankets closer, and goes back to sleep.
>
> Now his wife kicks him firmly and pushes him with both hands. "Go on. Close the window; it's cold outside."
>
> Grumbling, he slides out of bed, shuffles to the window, and bangs down the open lower half. Glaring at his wife he says, "So now it's warm outside?"

The husband takes his wife's reason—"It's cold outside"—as if it were the antecedent in a conditional, and reasons accordingly. I leave it to my friends and enemies to do the logic for all these examples. I will note only that sometimes the twisted reasoning is all there is to the joke, and sometimes that twist is tied to something else. Take this example:

> An elderly rabbi in Brooklyn, leader of a devout and observant congregation that meets in a tiny storefront converted into a synagogue, suffers the greatest calamity that can befall a pious man: his faith begins to waver. The more he reads of worldly disasters in the newspapers, the more his congregation dwindles, and the more his own body gives in to age, the more he is beset by doubts concerning his own religious convictions.
>
> As he ponders his growing spiritual crisis it becomes ever clearer to him that if his faith is not misplaced, he deserves a visible sign of its validity. He

has been pious, he has been scrupulously observant, he has been unwavering through the decades of his life, and now, he reasons, in his time of doubt he has earned the reassurance that would ease his mind.

Thus persuaded, he considers what form this visible sign might take, and after weeks of serious reflection, he conceives what would be the maximally appropriate sign: he should win the New York State Lottery.

Once he has reasoned to this point he begins to fashion prayers that he recites alone, at first twice a day, then more often, and finally hourly. He says: "O Holy One, Blessed art Thou, *ha Shem,* I will strengthen in my devotion and retain my piety and indeed go to my grave a man of faith if only I should win the New York State Lottery."

For weeks and then for months he carries on in this way, adding this special lottery prayer to his regular agenda of Jewish observance, often continuing praying well into the evening, with no result. But he perseveres, both in fervor and in quantity, and finally, very late one night, he utters the prayer as he stands all alone in his synagogue. Suddenly he hears rumbling and observes a brilliantly pure light pervade the shabby building. As he feels the building itself begin to quake he hears a beautifully melodious voice seemingly coming from every direction saying,

"So *nu,* buy a ticket."[25]

In this joke, the rabbi is made to consider the Leibnizian question of whether even God can work a logical contradiction.

Sometimes the joke incorporates not a genuine contradiction, nor even an absurdity, but just a palpable implausibility. For instance,

Cruising on Fifth Avenue one day, a taxi is hailed by a man standing on the corner. Entering the cab, the man says, "Take me to the Palmer House."

25. Heard during a lecture by Moshe Waldoks.

"The Palmer House?" says the cabbie. "That's in Chicago."

"I know," says his fare. "That's where I want to go."

"I'll drive you to Kennedy," says the cabbie. "You can fly."

"I'm afraid of flying."

"Then I'll drive you over to Grand Central and you can take the train."

"No, the train takes too long and besides, then I'd have to get from Union Station to the Palmer House."

"If I drove you all the way to Chicago it would cost a fortune. Twice a fortune, because you'd have to pay for me to deadhead back to New York."

"That's OK, I can afford it. Here's a few hundred dollars now. I'll pay the rest when we get there."

With no further argument to make, the cabbie drives out of Manhattan into New Jersey and then connects with the Pennsylvania Turnpike, thence to the Ohio Turnpike, the Indiana Turnpike, and finally the Skyway into Chicago. He takes Stony Island to 57th Street, where he turns onto Lake Shore Drive. He drives north as far as Congress, cuts over to Michigan Avenue, goes north again until he can pull over to Wabash, drives back one block south, and screeches to a stop in front of the Wabash entrance to the Palmer House—after two days and one night of nonstop driving.

The passenger peers at the meter, gives the cabbie several hundred dollars to cover the fare and a decent tip, and then opens the door to step onto the sidewalk.

Before anyone can close the door, two women who have been standing at the curb slide into the back seat. Before the startled cabbie can speak, one of the women says, "We want to go to an address on Flatbush Avenue."

"Uh-uh, lady," says the cabbie. "I don't go to Brooklyn."

Sometimes the "logic" is very keen, indeed:

> A poor Jewish man stopped at the home of a rich Jew-
> ish man to ask for a handout.
> "I don't just give away money," declared the rich
> man, "but I have a Gentile who mows my lawn and I
> pay him $20. *You* mow my lawn and I'll pay you $25."
> "Let the Gentile keep the job," says the poor Jew.
> "Just give me the $5."

When a joke involves logic running wild, the joke will present an absurdity—an absurdity in itself or an absurd response
to a normal overture or a kind of doubling of absurdity, as in

> A taxi driver from the Bronx dropped off a passenger
> one day and then immediately felt sicker than he had
> ever felt in his life. Fearing that he might be mortally
> ill, he drove immediately to Park Avenue, where he
> had seen signs for the offices of many doctors. Locat-
> ing such an office, the cabbie burst in demanding to
> be seen at once.
> The receptionist, fearing that the man might die, no-
> tified the doctor, and the doctor immediately saw the
> cabbie. After a few routine tests the doctor concluded
> that the cabbie was suffering only from indigestion,
> and indeed the cabbie was already beginning to feel
> better. "Thank you, doctor, thank you, thank you,"
> gushed the cabbie. "How much do I owe you?"
> "Just see my receptionist on your way out," said
> the doctor.
> At the reception desk the cabbie received the bill
> and discovered with horror that it was for $150.
> "$150," he shrieked, "that's highway robbery, that's
> outrageous, that's out of the question."
> The receptionist tried to calm the cabbie, begging
> him to be quiet and not disturb other patients, but
> to no avail. The man kept yelling and began to run
> around the room. Hearing the commotion from the
> outer office, the doctor came out. When the reception-

ist explained the trouble, the doctor turned to the cabbie and said, "Be quiet. I can't have all this disruption
here, with my patients waiting. Just pay whatever you
think you should and that will suit me."

"Sounds good," said the cabbie, "I think $15 is
right." With that he pulled out his wallet and ex-
tracted a ten and five ones.

The doctor took the bills and the cabbie turned to
leave. Before he reached the door the doctor said,
"You paid $15 and I'll settle for $15, but I want to ask
you: Park Avenue is the most expensive place in New
York for doctors, and you must know that. So why did
you come here?"

"Listen, doc, where my health is concerned, price
is no object."[26]

These last few jokes, logically speaking, all incorporate im-
plausibilities, absurdities, and downright contradictions. What
does it mean that one *laugh* at such a thing?

An absurdity can be an example, a symbol, or even, say, an
emblem of *incomprehensibility*. To laugh at an absurdity can be
an acceptance of incomprehensibility. An incomprehensible
thing is unsettling. It can be terrifying, but it need not be—
not if one can accept it, acknowledge it, live with it.

What is the most incomprehensible thing you know? What
about the world? What about just the part of the world that is
its people? Sometimes people do amazing, stupefying things,
leaving one with nothing to say but "Look what the bastards
are up to now." One might be horrified at what the bastards
are up to; but one might chuckle: one might laugh at something utterly unexpected and not altogether sensible when it
happens.

I believe that the Hebrew Bible presents one conception of

26. This joke is told in a slightly different version by Freud in his *Jokes
and Their Relation to the Unconscious*. I was unaware of Freud's version when I
learned this one. My friend Jerrold Levinson thinks Freud's version is better. I
disagree. Make your own decision.

decency in which the fully human, fully acceptable response to the mystification of the world is a laughing acceptance, a kind of spiritual embrace. This is surely not the only conception presented in that text, but it is there, in the books of Genesis and Exodus. Let me begin with the latter and its grim, sober, unlaughing central character, Moses. During the time when he is being selected for the task of delivering the people, Moses has this encounter:

> Now Moses, tending the flock of his father-in-law Jethro, the priest of Midian, drove the flock into the wilderness, and came to Horeb, the mountain of God. An angel of the Lord appeared to him in a blazing fire out of a bush. He gazed, and there was a bush all aflame, yet the bush was not consumed. Moses said, "I must turn aside to look at this marvelous sight; why doesn't the bush burn up?" When the Lord saw that he had turned aside to look, God called to him out of the bush: "Moses! Moses!" He answered, "Here I am."
>
> (Exodus 3:1–4)

There is certainly no laughter here, and surely there is nothing funny, but Moses' response expresses his capacity for a certain kind of response to the world, and in that capacity Moses has a quality that suits him to be God's choice. "I must turn aside to look at this marvelous sight," says Moses, and when he does turn aside, God judges him to have done something special. Not every human being turns aside to look at marvelous sights. This is implied in the fact of Moses' extraordinary suitability for God's purpose, a suitability detected in Moses when he turns aside to look at the bush. If a human being does not turn aside to look when a marvelous sight is available, there are two possible explanations: either the sight does not strike him as marvelous, or, however it may strike him, he does not care to look. In the first case he has no awareness of the marvelous in the world; in the second case he has no appreciation of it. Moses has both.

What is Moses' further response when he has turned aside to look? How does he regard the bush? We do not know. Would Moses merely sit and gaze into the endlessly burning bush? Would he undertake the physical chemistry necessary to attempt an explanation of this nonconsuming burning? We are not told what Moses would have done. He has no time for any response: God calls him as soon as he has shown his interest. And when a man like Moses is called by God, he answers, "Here I am." This is exactly the answer given by Abraham. Abraham makes this answer both to God and to his own son Isaac during the terrible time when Abraham is preparing to sacrifice Isaac. There is no hint of laughter in the episode called "The Binding of Isaac," but the Abraham who is tried there is a man capable of responses as extraordinary as those of Moses, and it is his "Here I am" that is echoed by Moses; and Abraham is intrinsically connected to the laughter of the book of Genesis. Here is that laughter:

> And God said to Abraham, "As for your wife Sarai, you shall not call her Sarai, but her name shall be Sarah. I will bless her; indeed I will give you a son by her. I will bless her so that she shall give rise to nations; rulers of peoples shall issue from her." Abraham threw himself on his face and laughed, as he said to himself, "Can a child be born to a man a hundred years old, or can Sarah bear a child at ninety?"

(Genesis 17:15–17)

Why is Abraham laughing? Exactly what is he laughing *at*? Is he laughing at the idea that a child might be born to a couple whose combined age is 190 years? Why is that idea laughable? Does Abraham think it is *impossible* that there be such a birth? No. Abraham might accept the possibility of such a birth, but he cannot *comprehend* it. Does this mean that Abraham has no faith? No: it means that he is a human being. Human beings are marked by their ability to understand, but as Kant insists, they are marked as well by the limits of what they can understand. Abraham cannot begin to *understand* how this birth could be. It is the same for Sarah, a woman who frequently understands more than her husband:

> [By the terebinths of Mamre] they said to him, "Where is your wife Sarah?" And he replied, "There, in the tent." Then one said, "I will return to you when life is due, and your wife Sarah shall have a son!" Sarah was listening at the entrance of the tent, which was behind him. Now Abraham and Sarah were old, advanced in years; Sarah had stopped having the periods of women. And Sarah laughed to herself [in the Septuagint she laughs aloud], saying, "Now that I am withered, am I to have enjoyment—with my husband so old?" Then the Lord said to Abraham, "Why did Sarah laugh, saying, 'Shall I in truth bear a child, old as I am?' Is anything too wondrous for the Lord? I will return to you at the time that life is due, and Sarah shall have a son." Sarah lied, saying, "I did not laugh," for she was frightened. But He replied, "You did laugh."

(Genesis 18:9–15)

The Lord says, "Is anything too wondrous for the Lord?" and the whole answer is, No, and nothing is too wondrous for Him to understand, but some things that He understands are indeed too wondrous for Sarah. Even Sarah, a woman whose faith is at least the equal of Abraham's and whose understanding sometimes outreaches his. And then why does the Lord insist on the fact of Sarah's laughter, insist upon having it acknowledged all round? Volumes deserve to be written about this, and I ask to make only this footnote. It is not at all clear that God disapproves of Sarah's laughter. He demands persistently that she admit that she laughed, and therein she acknowledges that God knows her laughter. One might say, as one might have said about Abraham, that were a woman or a man of perfect faith, then she or he would not laugh at God's ideas. I would not say that. I prefer to say that what Sarah is being shown—and what we are shown in Sarah—is that the most nearly perfect human faith and understanding are consistent with laughter. The perfect and most sober among you may disagree. There is no way to settle this from the text, but there is this:

> The Lord took note of Sarah as He had promised, and the Lord did for Sarah as He had spoken. Sarah conceived and bore a son to Abraham in his old age, at the set time of which God had spoken. Abraham gave his newborn son, whom Sarah had borne him, the name of Isaac. And when his son Isaac was eight days old, Abraham circumcised him, as God had commanded him. Now Abraham was a hundred years old when his son Isaac was born to him. Sarah said, "God has brought me laughter; everyone who hears will laugh with me."

(Genesis 21:1–7)

Isaac's name means 'laughter', but when Sarah says "God has brought me laughter," does she not also refer to the laughter God brought her when He told Abraham the birth would come and Sarah overheard? If so, then to say that Sarah ought not to have laughed is to say—or nearly—that God ought not to have brought her that laughter. Who would say that?

I will risk carrying this theme farther, even into one of the most difficult and painful passages in the Hebrew Bible, the passage Jews call the *Akedah,* the story of God's command to Abraham that he sacrifice his son Isaac. As you recall, when Abraham has followed the command right up to the point at which he will kill Isaac, God sends an angel:

> And Abraham picked up the knife to slay his son. Then an angel of the Lord called to him from heaven: "Abraham! Abraham!" And he answered, "Here I am." And he said, "Do not raise your hand against the boy, or do anything to him. For now I know that you fear God, since you have not withheld your son, your favored one, from Me." When Abraham looked up, his eye fell

upon a ram, caught in the thicket by its horns. So Abraham went and took the ram and offered it up as a burnt offering in place of his son. And Abraham named that site Adonai-yireh, whence the present saying, "On the mount of the Lord, there is vision."

(Genesis 22:10–14)

Volumes have been written about this passage. I believe the passage will remain troubling forever, for only a fool could think he had taken its measure in some interpretation. I am foolhardy enough to risk this slight addition to those volumes. If Isaac meant laughter when he was born, then does he not still mean that now, when God directs Abraham to sacrifice a ram but to free Isaac? Is not God Himself directing that laughter be freed and let loose in the world? Let us hope so.[27]

Like Moses, Sarah and Abraham confront marvels: a bush that burns without being consumed, a man of one hundred years who is fertile, a woman of ninety who gives birth. There are from time to time people who can take note of such things, who are alive to the wonders of the world. These things, in the cases at hand, are miraculous things, the signs and symptoms of God in the world. But they are also *absurd* things, things beyond the ken of those whose only apprehensions are literal, pedestrian, quotidian. For these people there are no truly absurd things, no things to be found in the world besides the predictable, retrodictable things of the canonical world. Their world is not the same as the world of Sarah or of Moses.

Whose world is it, anyway? Is it God's? How does the world strike God? If we turn, just for a moment, from the Bible to its massive rabbinical commentary, the Talmud, we find this. In this passage we read of a debate among scholars as to whether a cooking oven of a particular kind is ritually clean. Parts of

27. It might never have occurred to me to extend the Isaac/laughter theme past Isaac's birth and even on to his near-death at his father's hand if the possibility had not been pointed out to me by David Brent. He deserves credit for the idea, and I accept whatever blame is due someone who puts the idea into public print.

the passage are well known, but it is a wonderful passage, and
I will quote it all.

We learnt elsewhere: If he cut it into separate tiles,
placing sand between each tile: R. Eliezer declared it
clean, and the Sages declared it unclean; and this was
the oven of 'Aknai'. Why 'Aknai'?—Said Rab Judah in
Samuel's name: that they encompassed it with arguments as a snake, and proved it unclean. It has been
taught: On that day R. Eliezer brought forward every
imaginable argument, but they did not accept them.
Said he to them: 'If the *halachah* [religious law] agrees
with me, let this carob-tree prove it!' Thereupon the
carob-tree was torn a hundred cubits out of its place—
others affirm, four hundred cubits. 'No proof can be
brought from a carob-tree,' they retorted. Again he said
to them: 'If the *halachah* agrees with me, let the stream
of water prove it!' Whereupon the stream of water
flowed backwards. 'No proof can be brought from a
stream of water,' they rejoined. Again he urged: 'If the
halachah agrees with me, let the walls of the school-
house prove it,' whereupon the walls inclined to fall.
But R. Joshua rebuked them, saying: 'When scholars are
engaged in a *halachic* dispute, what have ye [*sic*] to in-
terfere?' Hence they did not fall, in honour of R. Joshua,
nor did they resume the upright, in honour of R.
Eliezer; and they are still standing thus inclined. Again
he said to them: 'If the *halachah* agrees with me, let it be
proved from Heaven!' Whereupon a Heavenly Voice
cried out: 'Why do ye dispute with R. Eliezer, seeing
that in all matters the *halachah* agrees with him!' But
R. Joshua arose and exclaimed: '*It is not in heaven.*' What
did he mean by this?—Said R. Jeremiah: That the Torah
had already been given at Mount Sinai; we pay no attention to a Heavenly Voice, because Thou hast long since
written in the Torah at Mount Sinai, *After the majority
must one incline.*

R. Nathan met Elijah and asked him: What did the
Holy One, Blessed be He, do in that hour? —He
laughed, he replied, saying, 'My sons have defeated
Me, My sons have defeated Me.'

(*The Babylonian Talmud, Seder Nezikin, Baba Mezia,*
chapter 4, 59a–59b [London: Soncino Press, 1935],
352–53; translation by H. Freedman)

The author of this passage has chosen to say that God
laughed. A very bold attribution. To gain some sense of the sensibility of the author we might compare the passage from the Talmud with this:

[Our rulers] must not be prone to laughter. . . .
Then if anyone represents men of worth as overpow-
ered by laughter we must not accept it, much less if
gods [are represented laughing].

That is Plato's Socrates speaking, in the *Republic* (388d). His
admonition represents a clear, recognizable, admirable sensibility. It is at odds, however, with the passages from the Bible
and the Talmud. First we have the Bible representing a man of
worth—if Abraham is not a man of worth, the Bible knows
none—laughing, and now we have an ardent student of the
Bible and of people and of the world daring to say that not just
a god but the one true God laughs. Why does the author say
that about God? Why does he report that Elijah witnessed God
laughing? Well, first, what would a man or woman say about
the event in question? A group of scholars are debating the law,
to determine what is God's will as it is expressed in the law.
Given absolutely unmistakable indications of God's own opinion in the matter, they proceed to disregard it and reach a de-
termination of God's will that contradicts God's explicit decla-
ration. I say that they have committed a kind of absurdity, and
I laugh. Elijah reports that so did God. Well, what else was He
to do?

It is a strain for some people to think that there might be a

Jewish kind of laughter or that it is a particularly Jewish thing
to laugh. Nietzsche, for instance, says this:

> Verily, that Hebrew died too early whom the preachers
> of slow death honor; and for many it has become a ca-
> lamity that he died too early. As yet he knew only tears
> and the melancholy of the Hebrew, and hatred of the
> good and the just—the Hebrew Jesus: then the longing
> for death overcame him. Would that he had remained
> in the wilderness and far from the good and the just!
> Perhaps he would have learned to live and to love the
> earth—and laughter too.
>
> (*Thus Spoke Zarathustra*, First Part, "On Free Death," in
> the Walter Kaufmann translation)

As so often with Nietzsche, he has about as much right as
he has wrong, and he is excruciating in both parts. It is remarkable about Jesus that he never laughed, although it might be
equally important to note that Jesus' biographers chose never
to portray him laughing. Is it the Hebrew in him that keeps
Jesus melancholy and unlaughing? What could be more Hebrew than those passages from the Bible and the Talmud? Mat-
thew, Mark, Luke, and John do not recount any laughter from
Jesus. Had Jesus lived longer, had he become more Christian
and less Jew, would he have been more likely to laugh? The
laughter of the awestruck Abraham and Sarah does not come
forth from Jesus. Why not? Because he is a Hebrew?

Is it more Jewish than Christian or Greek to laugh? I have
absolutely no idea, not only no idea how to answer this question but also no idea what the question means. There is certainly a strain of Jewish thought that militates against laughter,
that associates laughter with a loss of seriousness, with the ab-
sence of gravity. At its best, this is a sobering, helpful stricture.
At its worst, which is more common, I think, it is a persistent
mistaking of ponderousness for seriousness.

And certainly there is Greek laughter, and Christian laughter, and Greek and Christian jokes. I have wanted to mark out

only one kind of joke and a kind of laughter that goes with that kind of joke, and to note for that laughter a sanction as serious as any the Hebrew tradition can bestow. Of course those jokes and that laughter are available to Christians, to Greeks, to all the nations.

However undignified laughter can be, and surely Plato was right to think that sometimes it can be utterly undignified, the fact of laughter in the world is surely of note, and I am scarcely the first to feel a sacred twinge in someone's laughter. Christopher Fry, for instance:

THOMAS.
Are you going to be so serious
About such a mean allowance of breath as life is?
We'll suppose ourselves to be caddis-flies
Who live one day. Do we waste the evening
Commiserating with each other about
The unhygienic condition of our work-cases?
For God's sake, shall we laugh?

JENNET.
For what reason?

THOMAS.
For the reason of laughter, since laughter is surely
The surest touch of genius in creation.
Would *you* ever have thought of it, I ask you,
If you had been making man, stuffing him full
Of such hopping greeds and passions that he has
To blow himself to pieces as often as he
Conveniently can manage it . . . would it also
Have occurred to you to make him burst himself
With such a phenomenon as cachinnation?
That same laughter, madam, is an irrelevancy
Which almost amounts to a revelation.

(Christopher Fry, *The Lady's Not for Burning,* Act II)

I am doing my best with the jokes recounted in this book, and I am very fond of nearly all of them, but I am not claiming them to be sacred. What I claim is that Abraham, Sarah, and those of us who laugh at these jokes are all laughing at the same kind of thing. It is something not fully comprehensible, and our laughter is an acceptance of the thing in its incomprehensibility. It is the acceptance of the world, of a world that is endlessly incomprehensible, always baffling, a world that is beyond us and yet our world.

This laughter is akin to God's laughter Itself, as He observed His children doing the damnedest things. The world and its inhabitants are forever doing the damnedest things. It is one Jewish mode of acceptance and appreciation to receive these things in their wonder. Then this laughter may be heard as the echo of faith. I mean to include laughter at those jokes. Does it offend you to have the prediction of the birth of Isaac compared with "Uh-uh, lady, I don't go to Brooklyn"? Perhaps it seems to you an absurd comparison. If so, then you can pass me off as saying the damnedest things.

Jews have no monopoly on jokes, nor on good jokes, nor even on jokes of a particular kind, and yet there is a characteristic association of Jews with a certain joking spirit, and that spirit has become an aspect of American joking. I would like to say something about that, although it seems to me impossible to be precise. It is surely not possible to *define* Jewish humor, but it may be possible to say something about what it is, and I will risk two very general observations: (1) it is the humor of *outsiders;* (2) it exploits a deep and lasting concern and fascination with logic and language.

As examples of both characteristics we may think of Marx Brothers movies. (1) In these movies, we find an externally based, often subversive view of early-twentieth-century America, as seen by a not-too-recently-arrived immigrant (Groucho, who tends to wear very fancy, if goofy, American clothing, and speaks with no accent); a recent arrival (Chico, who wears strange, ill-fitting clothing and speaks with a ridiculous pseudo-Italian accent); and an arrival so recent that America still stupefies him so that he cannot speak at all (Harpo). If this iconography of the Marx Brothers is right—and I think it is (and I should admit that I have taken some of it from Moshe Waldoks)—then one should note that it is not specifically Jewish, but it is specifically outsider humor, particularly the humor of those who are outsiders because they are immigrants in this country. Here is the place to offer what may be the best idea in this book, and to say that I owe it entirely to my wife, Andy Austin Cohen. She is herself as Gentile as they come in this country, a genuine, authenticated WASP. It is she who has explained to me that WASPs themselves have become outsiders in this country, of which they were once the very essence of the inside, and that indeed—and here is her point—that just about all Americans are (or were, or will be) outsiders in this country. Her marvelous insight is that this may explain why it is that Jewish humor has flourished so in this country above all others. If it is the humor of outsiders, then what possibly better audience could there be than an audience composed entirely of outsiders, even if many of those other outsiders are out on different sides?

Jewish humor is not American humor, and American humor is not Jewish humor, and yet America and its Jewish jokers have been especially well suited to one another. I am not the first to note this, nor am I able to give the best explanation of this curious convergence. Here is W. H. Auden's observation, and his explanation.

If one compares Americans with Europeans, one might say, crudely and too tidily, that the mediocre American is possessed by the Present and the mediocre European is possessed by the Past. The task of overcoming mediocrity, that is, of learning to possess instead of being possessed, is thus different in each case, for the American has to make the Present *his* present, and the European the Past *his* past. There are two ways of taking possession of the Present: one is with the help of the Comic or Ironic spirit. Hence the superiority of

American (and Yiddish) humor. The other way is to
choose a Past, i.e., to go physically or in the spirit to
Europe.

("The American Scene," in *The Dyer's Hand and Other
Essays,* [New York: Random House, 1962], 321)

Auden thinks that both American and Jewish humor are
conspicuously good at doing what he calls taking possession
of the Present. To begin explaining why they go together so
well, one might consider this: America is nothing if not *new,*
and, as trite as it may be to repeat it, Americans are the children of the West. Among those children, perhaps the oldest are
the Jews, for they claim a memory going back to shortly after
Creation. In America, Jews are the outsiders of the outsiders,
and they are those with the longest history of being outsiders,
and they have learned to occupy that position. When I tell the
story of Berl debating the Jesuit, I feel as old as Abraham, and
when I come to the story's twisting, doubling humor, I feel as
young as a baseball rookie.

So much for the first point, that Jewish humor is the humor
of those standing outside, somewhat detached from the object
being observed. That is a point about the posture or stance of
Jewish humor. But what about the content of the humor, what
are its "stylistic" characteristics? I have said that it has to do
with an intense concentration on logic and language. For an
illustration I turn again to the Marx Brothers.

(2) In *Monkey Business,* Groucho speaks a line worth a
monograph of commentary. Lucille (played by Thelma Todd)
says to Groucho, "You can't stay in that closet," and Groucho
replies, "Oh, I can't, can I? That's what they said to Thomas
Edison, mighty inventor . . . Thomas Lindberg, mighty flier,
and Thomas Shefsky, mighty like a rose. . . ."[28]

The move from 'Thomas Edison' to 'Thomas Lindberg' to

---

28. This is one of the few instances in which the Marx Brothers' Jewishness
creeps overtly into their movies, along with "Hooray for Captain Spaulding,
the African explorer, did someone call me 'shnorer'? . . ."

'Thomas Shefsky' is very Marxian. As is a much later tribute to the Marx Brothers, in Woody Allen's *Casino Royale:* When someone tells Woody that he is crazy, he replies, "That's what they said about Einstein." His critic says that nobody ever said that about Einstein, and Woody replies, "They would have, if he had carried on this way." Virtually anyone hearing this exchange is bound to think of the Marx Brothers, although Groucho's line is so much more complex it approaches sublimity. After seizing on 'Thomas' as the preferred first name of American greats (although he never mentions Thomas Jefferson, an obvious real Thomas he might have named), Groucho goes on to denominate Tomashefsky a great American by reconstructing the name of the Yiddish-theater great, and then solidifies this identification by linking Tomashefsky to a popular American song ("Mighty Like a Rose").

These two things, the insane logic and the maniacal moves through language, are abiding features of Jewish humor. They are present in many of my own favorite Jewish jokes. Here is an example.

> The Soviet Union at last decides to take commemorative note of Lenin's time in Zurich. This has the significance, after all, of Jesus' ordeal in the desert and Moses' stint on Sinai.
>
> The principal artifact of the celebration is to be a painting, to be called *Lenin in Zurich,* and a young Leningrad painter is commissioned. Some older members of the party are troubled by the fact that the painter is Jewish, but they are reassured by younger colleagues who note, after all, that the time is long past when one of Mikhail Turovsky's paintings was removed because its subject looked too Jewish, and surely this sort of thing is no longer a concern in the Soviet state, and besides, this painter doesn't even know of Turovsky.
>
> The commission is given a year in advance, and for the whole twelve months the painter works secretly.

Finally comes the inaugural of the new holiday, and
the painting is hung, draped with a cloth, on its appointed spot in the Kremlin.

The Red Army Band plays, the Red Army Chorus
sings, the Red officials speak, and then the cloth is
pulled away.

In stunned horror and outrage the spectators gaze
upon the painting, in which are to be seen Krupskaya
[Mrs. Lenin] and Trotsky, together in bed, between
them wearing no more than Trotsky's pince-nez.

Cries ring out, a rumble is heard, and nothing is
clearer than the insistent question "Where is Lenin?"
The painter steps forward and replies,

"In this painting, Lenin is in Zurich."[29]

This joke strikes me as typically "Jewish," and it would continue to do so even if the painter were not identified as Jewish,
and in this regard it resembles the jokes included earlier, in the
remarks on the traditional sanction for Hebrew humor. Like
them, it displays an interest in absurdity, and this one makes
even clearer that there is an interest in absurdity as it appears
in the logic of language.

Where does this obsession with language and its logic come
from? I have often heard and read that it is an important fact
about the genesis of Jewish humor in America that its practitioners and its first audience were bilingual. And so they
were, many of them coming to America already knowing Yiddish and perhaps Polish or Russian or German, and then learning English. But something like that was true of all immigrant
groups except those from Britain. There has to be something
else, something added to the concern with language. I do not
minimize the importance of this bilingualism. Nothing is as
likely to draw one's attention to the fascinations of language as

29. Peter Dembowski, a very shrewd student of jokes, tells me that this is
quintessentially an eastern European joke of the kind found in Poland, and
that this is further evidence of a convergence in sensibility between Jews and
Poles. I think he is right.

undertaking to learn another language. (It is a commonplace that many of us American native English-speakers first realized anything significant about English syntax and semantics when we first tried learning another language.) But practitioners of Jewish humor must have been drawing on something else, and that something else led to the crazy reasoning so often present.

I think the something else must be the Jewish tradition (or traditions) of reasoning and argument developed in the study of Jewish texts. Here we have centuries of inference from principles, attempts to locate principles for conclusions already at hand, the selective citation of authority, the subversion of authority—all of this almost always presented as sequences of argument. Sometimes the arguments are deductive, sometimes dialectical, sometimes by analogy, sometimes in terms of metaphors. At times this practice has been so continuous and so intense that it has needed to burst its own bonds in displays of self-parody. Something of a commentary is this story:

> A young man applies to study with a Talmudic scholar. The scholar rejects him, saying, "Before you can study Talmud, you must know Jewish logic."
>
> "But I already know logic," protests the student, "Aristotelian syllogisms, truth-functional logic, predicate logic, set theory, everything."
>
> "That's not Jewish logic," replies the scholar, but the student persists, and so the scholar offers to give him a test to determine whether he is prepared.
>
> "Here is the question," says the scholar. "Two men go down a chimney. One has a dirty face, one has a clean face. Which one washes?"
>
> "That's easy," says the student, "the one with the dirty face."
>
> "Wrong," says the scholar. "The one with the clean face looks at the other one, sees a dirty face, and thinks his must also be dirty, and so the one with the clean face washes."
>
> "I see," says the student. "It is a little more compli-

cated than I thought, but I can do this. Please test me again."

"All right," sighs the scholar. "Here is the question. Two men go down a chimney. One has a dirty face, one has a clean face. Which one washes?"

In surprise the student answers, "Just as you said, the one with the clean face washes."

"Wrong," says the scholar. "The one with the dirty face observes his companion looking at him and making ready to wash his face. 'Ah ha,' he thinks. 'He must see a dirty face, and it's mine.' And so the one with the dirty face washes."

"It is even more complicated than I yet realized," says the student, "but now I do understand. Please test me once more."

"Just once more," says the scholar. "Here is the question. Two men go down a chimney. One has a dirty face, one has a clean face. Which one washes?"

"Now I know the answer," says the student. "The one with the dirty face washes, just as I thought in the beginning, but for a different reason."

"Wrong," says the scholar. "If two men go down a chimney, how can only one have a dirty face? Go and study. When you know Jewish logic, come back."

It is the essence of this tradition that these debates, these arguments—let us call it 'this study'—goes on and on. Of course resolutions are found, consensus develops, and not everyone's opinion is of equal weight. But there is no systematic finality. In a word, there is no Pope. (Perhaps this is why there are few Jesuit standup comics.) A person in this tradition does not only learn and memorize the conclusions reached, although he must do some of that. Rather, he joins this study: he argues, debates, contests, criticizes, and learns; and he does not stop. It is possible to be so consumed by this study that one loses one's bearings.

"Why should 'eretz' be spelled with a gimmel?"
"A gimmel? It isn't."

"Why shouldn't 'eretz' be spelled with a gimmel?"

"Why *should* 'eretz' be spelled with a gimmel?"

"That's what I'm asking you—Why should 'eretz' be spelled with a gimmel?"[30]

So much for this study, which I am taking as a tradition somehow standing behind the abiding characteristic of at least some Jewish humor, namely the fascination with language and logic. This is a kind of Jewish style, and I offer it as a partial elaboration of the second point, the one about the characteristic form of Jewish humor. My first point was that Jewish humor has often been the humor of outsiders. The two points do go together, I think. When one has this tradition of incessant questioning and criticizing, then when one finds oneself an outsider, one will deploy these techniques of criticizing and questioning when examining what is inside.

It is a mistake to take this critical humor as giving a simply negative appraisal of what it seems to be directed at. In fact it is a double mistake. In the first place, it is not such an entirely negative appraisal. In the second place, it is not directed only at the inside. Think of the Marx Brothers again. (It is almost always worth thinking of the Marx Brothers.) Yes, they are showing the ridiculous aspects of country mansions, of fancy race tracks, of opera (and especially of opera in America), and of all the rest. But Harpo loves most of this stuff, and Groucho is moving rapidly to become an insider. And it is not only the rich matrons and Italian operas that are shown as ridiculous. The Marx Brothers themselves are displaying their own utter and complete ridiculousness.

Jokes directed at oneself and one's own are vital, and fascinating. They are a species of subversive joke, but how far can one go in subverting oneself and still be oneself? When the honest but troubled Freud, the smug Marx, and the peevish and puerile Wittgenstein make their negative remarks about Jews, are they being non-Jewish or are they being even more

---

30. Stanley Cavell, who has a deep appreciation of the wonder of this dialogue, and of many other things, tells me that he has seen important philosophers transfixed by the exchange.

Jewish than ever? Here is a story about the activity of subversion meant to register its limits.

> Once a perverse young Jewish man in a small village in Poland enjoyed his role as *apikoros* [see appendix]. But after some time annoying his fellow villagers, he decided he needed to expand his talents, and so he took himself off to study with the man he had heard of as "the great *apikoros* of Warsaw." After arriving in Warsaw he found the man in question and followed him around for many days, observing what he did. Then he approached the man, saying, "I don't see that you are such a great *apikoros*. You observe the holidays, you attend *shul*, you keep a kosher house. I am already a better *apikoros* than you."
>
> "Oh?" inquired the older man, "what do you do?"
>
> The young man replied proudly, "I sneak *treif* into the butcher shop, I rearrange the pages of the *siddur*, I re-roll the Torah scrolls so that the wrong portions are read. Things like that."
>
> "I see," said the older man. "Let me tell you: I'm an *apikoros*; you're a *goy*."

Let me end this little analysis now, with the hypothesis that what lies behind at least one strand of Jewish humor in America are these two characteristics of the humorists: they have the stance of an outsider, and the soul of a critical student. A tendency to laugh at absurdity and to traffic in jokes exploiting this tendency are constituents in American laughter generally, I think, and they may well have their own sources there, but surely they have been abetted by the infiltration of Jewish humor.

6

TASTE, MORALITY, AND
THE PROPRIETY OF JOKING

DO I THINK WE *SHOULD* JOKE about absurdities? Should we be laughing at the fact of death? Death is a bleak topic. Jokes about death can be bleak. But apart from all that bleakness, joke-telling about death has a special dark side, which it shares with much joke-telling. I am one of those who believe jokes and joke-telling are wonderful and can be very serious, but I am also aware of the danger in too much joke-telling and joke-telling when it is out of place. Whether joking is in place or out of place may depend upon who is telling jokes to whom. In this regard, at least in America, or at least in my part of America, there seems to be a difference between men and women. Although it is not true uniformly and universally, men are much more likely to tell jokes to one another than are women to tell jokes to one another. Men are probably more often joke-tellers than women, and when women do tell jokes, they are more likely to tell them to men than to women. Why is that? Perhaps women have other conversational devices for establishing and maintaining intimacy, while for at least some men, joke-telling is a primary device of this kind.[31] But joking is almost always out of place when it is a kind of avoidance. Telling a joke about death can be a way of dealing with death, even of grappling with it; but sometimes the only proper way to think about death is to try looking it straight in its morbid, mordant eye, and on those occasions telling a joke is exactly the wrong thing to do because it is a way of avoiding the real issue. People like me who tell too many jokes, and tell them too often and in too many kinds of situations, usually get away with it because the laughter and ostensible humor are taken to

31. I owe this point to Andy Austin Cohen, herself a joke-teller, and an excellent audience to tell jokes to, who tells many more to men than to women.

be good things, things worth having even at the cost of other
things. But we shouldn't get away with it, because a laugh
is not always worth it, not if it is a deflection from something
else that needs to be done. Mark Twain knew a very great deal
about these matters, but when he said "Against the assault of
laughter nothing can stand," he neglected to note that some
things should remain standing.

When is it in order to joke about death, and when not? I
cannot say. No one can say. There is no rule here. It is up to
you every time, it is up to you and your own moral sensibility
(which includes concern for the sensibilities of others) to decide whether to tell a joke or to get serious, or whether, perhaps, telling a joke is a way of getting serious. This is a fact
about all joke-telling, whether the jokes are about death or
about anything else.

Here are two principles: One, jokes cannot be the entire human response to death, or to anything else; two, any total response to death that does not include the possibility of jokes
is less than a totally human response.

Sometimes a joke is exactly the wrong response, the wrong
overture to make. But when is this? If those jokes about New
York and New Jersey are acceptable and are not seriously offensive, this one is a bit different.

> When God was creating the world, when He was fin-
> ishing Europe He realized that France had come out
> perfect, which was not His plan. So He made
> Frenchmen.

However you feel about these jokes yourself, I think you
know this: it would be surprising if New Yorkers or New
Jerseyites were upset about the man from Nebraska or the rec-
itation of the alphabet, but it would not be surprising if
Frenchmen (and maybe others) were annoyed by this joke.
But what is the difference? If, as I think, there is no formula to
tell us which jokes are offensive or when it is the wrong time
to put forth a particular joke, it may be possible to say something about just what goes wrong when these transgressions

occur. To start, it will be useful to take a look at almost everyone's favorite example of jokes that shouldn't be told, "ethnic
jokes."

In one kind of so-called ethnic joke, the ethnicity of the
characters is not essential to the joke, because identifying someone as a Pole, or a Sikh, or an Iowa legislator is simply to stipulate that the character is inept or stupid or benighted. There is
no doubt considerable significance in the fact of just which
groups are chosen to be used in this way, and there may be
moral, political, or social objections to using these groups in
this way, but their ethnicity itself does not function in the joke.
In other jokes, also deservedly called ethnic jokes, the ethnicity itself (or the religion or the nationality) is a substantial
element in the joke. Here is an Irish joke (which is also an
English joke, to a degree):

> An out-of-work Irishman went walking around Lon-
> don until he found a construction site with a sign an-
> nouncing that workmen were being hired. When he
> applied for the job it was his bad luck that the fore-
> man in charge was an Englishman with a dismal view
> of the Irish.
>
> "So, Paddy, you think you can do the work?" asked
> the foreman.
>
> "Oh yes," said the Irishman. "I've been doin' con-
> struction for thirty years."
>
> "Then you really understand construction?" asked
> the foreman.
>
> "Of course," said the Irishman. "I can do it all—
> the plumbin', the electric, the carpentry."
>
> "Then you wouldn't mind if I gave you a bit of a
> test?" asked the foreman.
>
> "No, no. Test away."
>
> "Then tell me, Paddy, what is the difference be-
> tween a joist and a girder?"
>
> "It's too easy," said the Irishman. "'Twas the former
> wrote *Ulysses*, whilst the latter wrote *Faust*."

And here is a Polish joke (which is also a Russian joke, to a degree):

> In the days of the Cold War, long before the collapse of the Soviet Union, a Polish man let it be known to his friends that he kept his life savings, one hundred thousand zlotys, in his bed, under the mattress.
>
> In horror one of his friends objected, "It isn't safe there. You must put it in the bank."
>
> "Oh?" said the man, "and what if the bank fails?"
>
> "How could the bank fail? It is supported by the Polish government."
>
> "Oh?" said the man, "and what if the Polish government fails?"
>
> "How could our government fail? It is kept in place by the Soviet Union."
>
> "Oh?" said the man, "and what if the Soviet Union collapses?"
>
> "Wouldn't that be worth 100,000 zlotys?"[32]

In jokes like these, the relevant ethnicities are essential. Commonplaces about the Irish (that they are exceedingly and excessively literary), about the English (that they don't care much for the Irish), and about the Poles (that they are given to marvelously intricate subtleties and indirections of logic, and that they don't like Russians) are relatively very specific— quite different from just a generalized presumption that they are smart or stupid or venal. And in fact even if it were wrong it would not be unreasonable to believe that these commonplaces are in fact truths, whereas it is unreasonable to the point

---

32. I already knew this joke in 1985, when I was visiting my very good friends, a Polish colleague of mine and his wife, in Poland. During a splendid evening with my colleague, his wife, and various guests including his wife's mother, I told this joke. When I had finished, and the joke had been translated into Polish for general consumption, this older lady made a reply, also in Polish, that brought down the house, and I realized that my joke had been topped. My colleague translated for me, "She says it would be worth *200,000* zlotys." That was a rare moment. My colleague's mother-in-law has since died, but I will never forget her.

of utter ignorance to believe that Poles or Sikhs or students at Texas A&M are stupid.

An intermediate example is the joke in which an Englishman hears a joke about a monkey and a martini. Of course it is not true that the English have no sense of humor or appreciation of jokes, but it is nevertheless a kind of commonplace about them, and so the appreciation of the joke requires knowing this relatively specific commonplace.

I confess to a fondness for the structurally simplest kind of ethnic jokes, like

> **This year's Polish science prize went to an engineer in Warsaw who has developed a solar-powered flashlight.**

But I have a deeper appreciation for ethnic jokes in which the ethnicity is *used,* even if as slightly as in this:

> **A Polish man walks up to a counter and says, "I want to buy some sausage."**
>
> **"You want Polish sausage?" asks the clerk. "Kielbasa?"**
>
> **"Why do you think I want Polish sausage?" replies the man indignantly. "Why wouldn't I want Italian sausage, or Jewish sausage? Do I look Polish? What makes you think I'm Polish?"**
>
> **The clerk responds, "This is a hardware store."**

Here there is at least a reliance on the fact that there is such a thing as Polish sausage, even if the main presumption of the joke is the artificially given obtuseness of some group.

Sometimes the established presumption is not that the principal character is stupid or inept, but that he is disagreeable—mean, nasty, vicious. And sometimes that is all there is to the presumption, as in a number of jokes about agents and lawyers. For instance,

> **A man walked angrily into a crowded bar, ordered a drink, and then said to the bartender, "All agents are assholes."**

From the end of the bar a man spoke up, saying,
"Just a minute. I resent that."
"Why? Are you an agent?"
"No. I'm an asshole."[33]

In that joke nothing whatever is made of what might be
disagreeable about agents as such, nor is anything made of lawyers in this joke:

> You find yourself trapped in a locked room with a mur-
> derer, a rapist, and a lawyer. Your only hope is a re-
> volver you have, with two bullets left. What do you
> do?
> Shoot the lawyer. Twice.

Some jokes of this kind manage to invoke something at least
slightly more specific, as in

> One summer noontime two lawyers were walking to-
> gether over the Michigan Avenue bridge when they
> passed a particularly good-looking young woman in a
> thin summer dress walking the other way.
> "Man, I'd like to screw her," said one of the
> lawyers.
> His companion answered, "Yeah? Out of what?"

This joke suggests at least that lawyers' main interest is in
taking advantage of people, and that that ambition supersedes
any other interest they might take in human beings. It is possible, however, for such jokes, ones that presume to take an
ethnically or professionally or otherwise identified character as
the principal focus to make much more of the putative characteristics of the person. I have a preference for jokes that do

---

33. I owe this joke to Mrs. Billy Wilder, although she disclaims credit and
says she heard it from someone, perhaps Jack Lemmon. I owe it to Mrs. Wilder
because she told the joke to Karen Lerner, who gave it to me. I am further
indebted to Ms. Lerner for working keen improvements in the versions of some
of the jokes used in this book.

this, that make more of the presumed profession or ethnicity, and so I think that ethnic jokes like the one about the Irish workman who knows his Joyce and Goethe are, if not better, at least richer and subtler, and they are devices for achieving considerably greater intimacy. One reason is the same as the reason why I think color movies are better when the color is used for something, large-scale orchestral music is better when the extra instruments are used for more than simply increasing the volume, and fiction is better when all the characters have something to do with the story and are not added only as filler. I tend to have a better opinion of works of art, and to be further moved by them, when all their parts seem relevant. If the only point in making a character in a joke Polish is to signal that he will be inept, I have the feeling that some potential "material" in the joke has gone unused, and this seems somehow a waste.

Another reason for preferring a Polish or Irish joke in which it really matters that the character is Polish or Irish, is that such jokes require more of the hearer, involve him more intimately, and give him greater opportunity for self-congratulation in his appreciation of the joke. They invoke a bigger and richer contribution from the hearer. It is one thing to know, simply, that there are jokes in which Polish characters are found to do misguided things, even though such jokes can be very funny, and it is another thing, a more substantial thing, to know that Poles have a long-standing, historical distrust of Russia.

All of these jokes, the simpler and the more complex ones, feel innocuous, but they carry a hint of something unsavory.

It is a very widespread conviction, shared by me, that some jokes on some occasions, and maybe some jokes on all occasions, are, as we say, "in bad taste," and should be thought of as morally objectionable. But it is very, very difficult to say just what this moral defect is. First is the problem of finding a basis for any moral judgment passed upon fiction, and then there is the problem of establishing the impropriety of laughing at something, especially when the something is fictional. Fiction itself might be objectionable as such, for instance when one puts it forth in hopes of inducing a belief in something false, but surely this is not characteristic of jokes. I say this to you:

> A man was told by his doctor that to improve his health he should take up jogging, and he should run two miles every day. After a couple of weeks the man was to call the doctor to tell him how he was feeling. Two weeks later the man called and the doctor asked, "So how are you doing?"
>
> "I feel pretty good," said the man, "but I'm twenty-eight miles from home."

Would you object, and be angry with me because I had told you a falsehood? Ridiculous. (Of course even if there were such a misguided jogger, you might just find that funny.) Consider again this exquisite children's joke:

> What do Alexander the Great and Winnie the Pooh have in common?
>
> They have the same middle name.

Would you object to this that it is not true, that the word 'the' is not the middle name of either character, and, furthermore, that there is no such creature as Winnie the Pooh? Ridiculous. It cannot be an objection solely that the joke contains falsehoods. In fact, in many cases the entire joke is a falsehood. Actually, it is a *fiction,* and a fiction is not—simply—a falsehood. (And a joke is not—simply—a fiction.) Of course a fiction might be taken as a statement of fact, but the fiction is not itself accountable for that. And yet something disturbing appears in some jokes. Some people are bothered by this joke:

> A man calls home from his office one day, and his phone is answered by the maid, Maria. "Maria," says the man, "I'd like to speak to my wife."
>
> "I'm sorry, *señor,* but she cannot come to the phone. She is making love to a man in the master bedroom."

"My God, Maria. Can that be true?"

"Yes, *señor.* I am *muy* sorry."

"Maria, I must ask a favor. You have been with me many years, and now I need something from you."

"Yes, *señor,* what is it?"

"Maria, are you in my study?"

"*Sí, señor.*"

"In the upper right drawer of the desk you will find a loaded revolver. Take it to the bedroom and shoot them both."

The phone goes dead for a few minutes, and then Maria's voice comes through. "It is done, *señor.*"

"Good, Maria. I am in your debt. Now take the revolver, wipe off the handle, and throw it into the swimming pool."

"*Señor?* We have no swimming pool."

"Is this 555–4694?"

And, probably, more people are bothered by this one:

This year's annual prize for Polish medicine went to a surgeon in Krakow who performed the world's first appendix transplant.

But many more people are bothered by this one:

How did a passerby stop a group of black men from committing a gang rape?
He threw them a basketball.

Exactly what is *wrong* with any of these three jokes, and why is the last one so much more disturbing? The first is from a short-lived genre of "Maria jokes" that came from Southern California, I think (all such jokes involving a Mexican maid named Maria). The second is a Polish joke, so called, and the third is a black joke (although that category seems to me less well defined).

Each joke says that something happened, and in fact it didn't. There was no man who called home for his wife, got the wrong number without knowing it, and commissioned the murder of two strangers. There is no annual prize for Polish medicine, and no Polish surgeon performed an appendix transplant. No group of black men was distracted from a criminal sexual assault by being given the opportunity to play basketball.

But none of the jokes says that these things really happened. The jokes are short stories, fictions, perhaps, although of a very peculiar kind, and one can no more sensibly object to them as falsehoods than one might object to *Hamlet* that in fact there never was a prince of Denmark who had a couple of friends named Rosencrantz and Guildenstern.

Is it that the jokes say that Mexican maids are obtusely obedient even to the point of murder, that Poles are so stupid that they do not understand the point in organ transplant, that black men are sexually violent and mindlessly committed to playing basketball?

But the jokes don't *say* those things, any more than they say anything at all. Do they somehow purvey stereotypes, and disagreeable ones at that? Do those who respond to these jokes either believe in advance or come to believe nonsense about Mexican maids, Polish scientists, and black men? I doubt this. And I doubt that one could show any connection between traffic in such jokes and negative beliefs about these groups of people. Even if there is such a connection, I have myself been amused by all three jokes, and I do not myself believe any of those generalizations about the relevant characters, and yet these jokes disturb me, especially the last one, the one about criminal black basketball players. Why?

There are two questions. First I would like to know just why these jokes disturb me, and then I wonder whether my personal discomfort and objection can be generalized and rendered "objective" so that a negative assessment might be made about the jokes themselves. It may be that my personal dislike is just that—personal. This does not mean that it is unreal, that you should persist in telling me such jokes on the grounds that is only a personal, subjective matter that they do not agree with me, but it would mean that my complaint that such jokes are in bad taste or unwholesome comes to nothing more than my wish to be free of them. That is pretty much how it is for me, for instance, with regard to the music of Wagner and some of Eliot's poetry. I do not claim that these works are poor or corrupt, but only that I do not care for them; and if you do care for them, then this may mark a significant difference between you and me, but it signals nothing I am prepared to say about the works in themselves.

Why am I made uneasy about the joke about the black men? I think it is because I am made uneasy by the idea that black men are criminals and mindless basketball players. But how can an *idea* do that to me? Is it that I think the idea is false, or that it would lead to a false proposition if one believed it? But I think that almost all the statements and ideas presented in almost all the jokes I know are false in the sense that they would lead to false propositions if one believed them. Is there something especially disagreeable or obnoxious in this particular idea's being believed? Yes, I think so. If I, or others, believed in this idea, then I and others might well treat people badly. But so what? As a matter of fact I don't believe the idea, and I don't think that your telling me this joke leads either of us to believe the idea, nor does it suggest that either of us already believes it.

It is possible that the existence of such jokes and commerce in them are symptoms of pernicious attitudes and beliefs, and perhaps the jokes even are causes of this perniciousness. If that were true, then of course that would be the basis of a moral objection to the jokes. I do not know that this is true, and I do not know that it is false. And neither does anyone else know about this, nor does anyone have any idea how to discover whether it is true. But this question—the question of what role such jokes may play in bad behavior—might be set aside, if we could agree on how to answer a different question.

If jokes about the uncontrolled animalism of black men or about the venality of Jews could be shown to have no effect whatever on people's beliefs about black men and Jews, then would the jokes cease to be troublesome? I think the jokes would still be disturbing. Why? And need there be an answer to this question? Let me restart this little moral inquiry by asking, again, just what is disturbing in these jokes, as well as in certain works of art.

I do not like the portrayal of the Jewish nightclub-owners in Spike Lee's movie *Mo' Better Blues,* and I do not like the ridiculous portrayal of Jews in Edith Wharton's novel *House of Mirth.* No doubt this is at least partly because I am Jewish, but neither do I like the portrayal of black men in D. W. Griffith's movie *Birth of a Nation.* And why don't I like those portrayals? Because they are inaccurate? Because they are stereotypes? These seem lame answers to me.

I am not much bothered by the portrayal of WASPs in the movie *Auntie Mame,* although that portrayal is at least as inaccurate and unflattering as the others. It must be relevant that I do not regard WASPs as vulnerable, not in the way that Jews and blacks seem vulnerable. Is it that I am worried that people will think that Jews and blacks are in fact as they are portrayed in these works, and that I have no worry on behalf of the WASPs? It is not that I have no concern for WASPs; it is that I think they have nothing to worry about. But is that true? Are they not as entitled as anyone to object to stereotypical representations of themselves? Incidentally, stereotypes can be annoying, just as such, without regard to whether they are negative. In "Concerning the Jews," Mark Twain offers an exceedingly flattering characterization of Jews, and it troubles me almost as much as the negative portraits offered by T. S. Eliot and Edith Wharton. A stereotype can rob you of your particularity just as surely if it is flattering as if it is negative. What about the stereotype of young black men in that basketball joke?

The fact that this joke works is a fact only because of some genuine truths—not truths about black men, but truths about how black men are thought of. These truths are, for instance, that young black men are associated with basketball, and they are thought to have a passion for basketball that takes them away, for instance, from learning mathematics or learning to read; and that is what is being insinuated in a joke in which they give up even violent sex—another of their putative passions—for the chance to slam-dunk. I know all that, that these are associations that go with young black men, and it is only because I know all that that I am able to respond to the joke. Do I, perhaps, dislike it in myself that I know these things? And do I then dislike my own laughter at the joke? Is the joke working its magical establishment of intimacy by forcing me to acknowledge something I don't care for in myself? Would I rather that I did not know these things? Of course I wish that these were not things to be known, but is it my fault that they are, and that I know them?

If I were to offer some resounding moral condemnation of this joke, no doubt I would have to invoke some "moral theory," and then show that an implication of the theory is that this joke is Bad. I will not do that. It would be inappropriate in this book to do that, but I have another reason for not doing it: I think it can't be done.

A common, sometimes useful device in analytical, conceptual moral theory is the idea of an ideal creature, sometimes called an ideal observer, or an impartial spectator, or a person of practical wisdom. First, such a creature is characterized (perhaps as being completely informed, disinterested, and so on), and then it is supposed that the right way to act, or to feel, or to judge, is to act, feel, or judge as this ideal creature would. Try thinking up such a person, and then ask whether this person would disapprove of these jokes, whether he would tell them or laugh at them, and how he would feel about anyone who tells them. What do you think? Would he damn these jokes? I don't know, and neither, I think, do you.

Among contemporary normative theories of morality, most would require that it be shown that traffic in these jokes produces genuine harm to someone, or at least that it reduces the moral character of those who traffic in them. It seems to me preposterous to suppose that anyone could show that either of these consequences obtains. One of the more ponderous and depressing features of large-scale moral theories is that they tell you what makes things right or wrong, good or bad, and then leave it to you to take a case about whose morality you feel strongly and try to outfit it with the theory's sanctioned reasons. Thus someone who hates that joke about the black basketball players is forced to give his reasons for declaring it morally disagreeable. It may be that a mammoth raft of literature, propaganda, fiction, poetry, religious writing and preaching, and casual conversation can produce or sustain a general opinion of things, including an opinion of kinds of people— surely it would be foolish to deny that; but it is farfetched to indict a movie or a novel or a joke on those grounds. And worse: when it turns out that you can find no convincing evidence to support this claim about the effects of such jokes, you seem obliged to give up your moral complaint. And you shouldn't do that.

Here is some friendly advice: When you feel strongly that some joke (or anything else) is no damned good, and especially when you don't like having that joke told, and it seems to you that the thing—either itself or the telling of it—is morally defective, hold on to that feeling, and continue to express the feeling in terms of moral condemnation. When someone demands a moral-theoretical reason for your condemnation, ask them why they think you need one. You don't have to prove that a joke is funny, or that it is unfunny (good thing, too, because you couldn't do it), and surely you don't have to prove that it seems to you to be immoral. Do you have to prove that it is immoral? I don't think so. If your opponent thinks so, then ask him to supply the theory, the apparatus that would allow a claim that something is morally objectionable. When he does, then either you will be able to fit this joke to his theory, or you won't. If you can't make the theory work in support of your conviction, then try telling your philosophical opponent that you now have good reason to disbelieve his theory, namely that it can't account for the immoral character of this joke you hate. But before you do that, perhaps you should expand your categories. Not everything you dislike is illegal, or should be. Not everything you dislike is immoral. But something's being legal and morally acceptable doesn't mean you have to think it is OK. Nor does it mean you have to put up with it.

Don't like it, and don't put up with it when someone commits murder. Or when someone commits adultery. Or when young men don't give their seats to burdened women standing on the bus. Or when someone picks his nose. Or when people don't write thank-you notes for parties you have given or gifts you have sent. You don't have to put up with any of these. But don't suppose that there should be laws forbidding them, at least not all of them. And don't imagine that your dislike must be grounded in some stupefying Moral Theory.

You can avoid people who tell jokes you hate, or at least insist that they not tell them to you or when you are present. You can tell strong young men that they should give up their seats to pregnant women (although before doing this, you might well consider just what bus you are riding on).

Clarify these matters for yourself, and choose your words carefully—and above all be sure that they are *your words*—when you express your disapproval. This requires asking yourself persistently *why* you don't like something, as I tried to discover why I don't like the one about the black basketball players. Then notice whether you have felt a need for moral vocabulary.

I wish you good luck in thus maintaining your feeling of disgust—moral disgust, if that's how it feels to you—at the joke, but I insist that you not let your conviction that a joke is in bad taste, or downright immoral, blind you to whether you find it funny.

When an obnoxious portrayal is in a joke, it is likely to be upsetting in a special regard. Jokes are humorous, amusing, fun. It is ponderous and obtuse to object to the fun. The offended person who takes issue with a joke finds himself doubly assaulted, first by the offensive portrayal in the joke, and then again by the implicit accusation that he is humorless. But the offended person may make the reflexive mistake of denying that the joke is funny. More than once someone has demanded of me that I explain exactly why anti-Semitic jokes are not funny. I have come to realize that if there is a problem with such jokes, the problem is compounded exactly by the fact that they *are* funny. Face that fact. And then let us talk about it.

A young, earnest, white college student confesses his guilt at his own reactions when walking big-city streets after dark. He finds that he is more worried for himself when a stranger appears on the street when that stranger is black than he is when the stranger is white. He feels guilty for having this feeling, and he wishes he didn't feel that way. He is right to wish he didn't feel that way, if that is a wish that the world were different, but he is not wrong to have the feeling. Given the world as it is, there is nothing wrong with having the feeling, and it might well be a practical error not to have the feeling. As a matter of fact, given the neighborhood he walks in, it is enormously more likely that he will be set upon by a black stranger than by a white one. And that is a God-damned shame. But it is a fact. By all means, wish that it were not a fact. Weep because it is a fact. Try to change the world so that it will cease to be a fact. But don't turn away from the fact, don't force yourself to deny it.

Wish that there were no mean jokes. Try remaking the world so that such jokes will have no place, will not arise. But do not deny that they are funny. That denial is a pretense that will help nothing. And it is at least possible, sometimes, that the jokes themselves do help something. Perhaps they help us to bear unbearable affronts like crude racism and stubborn prejudice by letting us laugh while we take a breather.

What do you think of this joke?

The Secret Service has an opening in its ranks, needing to recruit someone to join those who guard the President of the United States. They post a notice in bulletins for government workers, and soon they receive three applications, one from an F.B.I. man, one from an agent from the Bureau of Alcohol, Tobacco, and Firearms, and a third from a Chicago city policeman. Each of the three is given a qualifying examination, beginning with the F.B.I. man.

The F.B.I. man is given a revolver and told to go into the adjacent room and shoot whomever he finds there. When he has been gone only a few minutes, the F.B.I. man returns, saying, "You must be out of your minds! That's my wife. I'm not shooting her."

"Fine," say the examiners. "You must be a good family man, but you're not cut out for the Secret Service."

Next the A.T.F. agent is sent in with the revolver, with the same instructions to shoot whomever he finds in the next room. He too returns in minutes, exclaiming, "That's the mother of my children, you lunatics."

"Good for you," say the examiners. "Enjoy your career in the bureau and continue looking after your wife; but we can't use you in the Secret Service."

Finally, the Chicago policeman is given the same test. When he has been in the adjacent room for about ten minutes, sounds are heard, the sounds of struggle and muffled groaning. A few minutes later the cop reappears, looking somewhat mussed, and says, "Some moron put blanks in the gun; I had to strangle her."

Now consider this: this marvelous story was told to me by my wife. She learned it from a Chicago policeman.[34] I do not know where the policeman came by it, but I do know that he and his fellow officers have had a good time telling it to one another. Do you think that is a bad thing? I don't. I don't know just what to make of it, but I do know that the dynamics of joking—including the intimacy sought and achieved, the relief gained from unpleasantness, and the moral dimensions of all this—depend absolutely upon who tells the joke and who

34. This was her good friend John Berry, a sergeant in the Chicago Police Department, an Irish-American, and the bearer of many a fine story.

hears it. Do you think this story *says* something about Chicago cops? If it does, it may well not be the same thing said when cops tell the joke to one another as it is when civilians tell the joke, and it is yet different when cops and civilians exchange this joke.[35] I think that Chicago cops' telling this joke to one another is a very good thing, a hopeful sign in a difficult world.

35. It is remarkable, I think, that Officers Golonka and Berry tell my wife, Andy Austin Cohen, the same jokes they exchange with other policemen.

APPENDIX

Throughout the text some jokes have been left unfinished, and some arcane jokes have been left unexplained. Here are the conclusions and some explanations.

PAGE 2 The Pope decides to have a garden made inside the Vatican, being unhappy with his private meditation garden, and so he asks for bids. He receives three, from a Polish gardener, an Italian gardener, and a gardener from Chicago. Each bidder makes his proposal in person.

The Polish gardener is the first to bid, and he says, "Your holiness, I am Polish like you, and I will make you a wonderful Polish garden, with dill, beets, Polish shrubbery, and everything. The cost will be only $600. That is $200 for the materials, $200 for the labor, and $200 for my profit."

"That is wonderful," says the Pope, "but I must listen to the other bidders."

The Italian gardener says, "Your holiness, I saw the Polish gardener who was just here, and I know you incline toward him, but let me tell you that it would be much better here in Rome for you to have a genuine Italian garden, and I can make one for you with tomatoes, oregano, basil, and all the rest, and the cost will be only $1,200. That is $400 for the materials, $400 for the labor, and $400 for my profit."

"Excellent," says the Pope. "You have a good plan, but I must listen to the final bidder."

The Chicago gardener comes in. "OK, Pope, I've got just what you need. Here are my credentials. A letter from my alderman, and he can get you letters from the mayor of Chicago, the head of the park district, and whatever you need. The cost will be $1,800."

"But wait," says the Pope, "you don't even tell me what kind of garden you will make, and why it should cost all of $1,800."

The Chicagoan replies, "Come on, Pope, it's $600 for you, $600 for me, and $600 for the Polish guy I'll hire to do the work."[36]

PAGE 2 A Jew was called to serve in the army. See pages 8–9.

PAGE 2 A priest in a small parish in the south of Ireland feared that paganism had appeared among his parishioners. Before undertaking to extirpate it, he thought he should first be sure, and so one Sunday, just as Mass concluded, he asked the congregation to remain for a few minutes while he asked some questions.

"How many of you," he asked, "have ever seen a ghost?"

The entire congregation raised their hands, and now the priest truly was concerned. He went on,

"And how many of you have ever talked to a ghost?"

About half the assembly raised their hands, and so the priest continued,

"How many of you have ever touched a ghost?"

Now only a third or so of the parishioners raised their hands, and the priest said he had only one more question.

"How many of you have ever had carnal knowledge of a ghost?"

Now, at last, no hands were raised. Except, that is, for Flynn, the village inebriate and layabout, who waved his hand from the back of the church.

"Flynn," said the priest, "get down here to the altar."

Flynn shambled to the front of the church, and the priest addressed him:

"Now, Flynn, you're on your honor, talkin' to me, a priest of God, and I ask you again, is it true that you've had intimate relations with a ghost?"

"Oh no, Father, I thought you said a goat."

36. According to Haskel Levi, this joke was told to him by William McCready, but this particular, brilliant elaboration, so far as I know, is due to Mr. Levi.

PAGE 2 How many Christian Scientists does it take to change a lightbulb?

Only one. He prays for the old bulb to come back on.

PAGE 2 A Sikh walked into a travel agency in New Delhi.

See page 10.

PAGE 2 How does an Irishman build a house, drink a Guinness, drive a car?

These are questions for exercise purposes. Find your own answers. It may help to recall the Englishman who committed suicide by ordering his chauffeur to drive over a cliff.

PAGE 2 How many Poles does it take to change a lightbulb?

Three. One holds the bulb while the other two turn the ladder he is standing on.

PAGE 2 How many psychiatrists does it take to change a lightbulb?

Only one, but he has to wait for the lightbulb to be ready to change.

PAGE 3 How many Jewish mothers does it take to change a lightbulb?

Don't worry, it's all right, I can sit here in the dark.

PAGE 3 As it happens, this is not only a golf joke, an Irish joke, and a leprechaun joke, but also a priest joke.

An Irish golfer hooked his drive into the woods. When he went to look, he couldn't find his ball, but he captured a leprechaun. When offered the customary three wishes, the man said he would like (1) to be a very good golfer, (2) to have plenty of money, and (3) to have a more gratifying sex life.

The following year the Irishman was walking in the woods one evening when he chanced upon the same leprechaun. When they had renewed their acquaintance, the leprechaun asked if the man's wishes had been met.

"Well, it's all fine," said the Irishman. "I've been a par golfer ever since I met you."

"Good," said the leprechaun. "And the money?"

"Unbelievable," said the Irishman. "No matter how much I've spent, I always find a new five-pound note in my pocket."

"That's fine, too," said the leprechaun. "And your sex life?"

"Great," said the Irishman. "I have a fine evening three or four times a month."

"What?" asked the leprechaun. "That's all? That's the best I did?"

"It's perfect," said the Irishman, "not bad at all for a priest."[37]

PAGE 3 How many members of the Spartacist Youth League does it take to change a lightbulb?

Five. One to change the bulb while the others yell "Smash darkness!"[38]

PAGE 9 For the two-men-going-down-a-chimney story, see page 65.

PAGE 16 What did Lesniewski say to Lukasiewicz?

Lesniewski and Lukasiewicz were two eminent logicians. And they were both Polish.

PAGE 16 What is a goy?

'Goy' in Yiddish or Hebrew means a non-Jew. For references to Nelson Goodman's introduction of the terms 'grue' and 'bleen' as alternatives to 'blue' and 'green', see my "Metaphor and the Cultivation of Intimacy," *Critical Inquiry* 5/1 (Autumn 1978): 1–13.

PAGE 16 The *Iliad* and the *Odyssey* were not written by Homer, but by some other Greek with the same name.

Besides his being Greek, the only facts known about Homer are that he wrote the *Iliad* and he wrote the *Odyssey*. It is thus unclear what it could mean for the author of those poems to be not Homer, but some other Greek Homer. What could make him an *other* Homer?

PAGE 17 I told my husband to buy all the stock in Pfizer he can find.

Viagra is a drug thought to increase male potency. Pfizer is the company that markets Viagra. If you needed to be told these things,

---

37. I owe this complex construction to my mother, Shirley Cohen, who has always had a rich sense of humor, and of late has taken an interest in jokes about clergymen and their religions. It was she who told me that Protestants do not recognize the Pope, Jews do not recognize Jesus, and Mormons do not recognize one another in liquor stores.

38. This fine realization is the invention of Stephen Melville.

you should spend less time reading books and more time paying attention.

PAGES 25, 62   Berl-in-debate-with-the-priest. Here it is. Be grateful.
   Around the turn of the century a Polish nobleman cultivated his
interest in theology. He heard of a certain Jesuit theologian reputed
to be the best debating scholar in all of European Christendom, and
by various inducements succeeded in bringing this learned man to
his estates. Near the center of the nobleman's vast holdings was a
small Jewish village. The prince sent word to the village that there
was to be a debate, a learned quarrel concerning theological matters, whose contending participants were to be the newly arrived
Jesuit and some Jew from the village. The village was instructed to
choose a champion and send him to the castle at the appropriate
time.
   This instruction was something of a nuisance for the village, but,
as always, they thought it best to placate their Polish landholder,
and so they set about deciding whom to send. While they were making this decision, another message came from the prince explaining
the format of the debate.
   The debate would be held, said the prince through his messenger, in the traditional manner, with each participant asking a question of the other until one debater was unable to answer. This would
end the debate with the asker of the question declared winner
and the one who was unable to answer declared loser. Furthermore,
said the messenger, the loss would be emphasized, again in the
traditional manner, by the prince's axman, who would decapitate
the loser.
   The villagers apprehended this new message with considerable
alarm. Preferring not to risk the head of any villager, even with the
possible reward of a decapitated Jesuit, they sent the prince a reply.
They conceded the debate, they said: the Jesuit should be declared
winner without even a contest.
   Soon the prince's messenger reappeared in the village. The
prince was determined that there should be a theological spectacu-
lar wherein was exhibited the superiority of Christianity to Judaism, and if there could be no civilized debate, then the prince would
have to send various emissaries into the village with the purpose of
carrying out a slight theological pogrom.
   The village was in a hopeless quandary. The elders realized at
once that unless someone was sent to debate the Jesuit, they would

have more to fear than a single decapitation. But that single decapitation was a certainty: there were no men of learning in the village, no scholars, certainly no theological debaters. But someone would have to go—never to return. The elders set about casting lots among themselves to choose a martyr, but before they finished they were approached by Berl, a poor, ignorant villager who earned his small livelihood mostly through the charity of the village. "I will go," he said.

The elders were astonished, for, as one of them said, "You, Berl, who did not complete even two years of elementary Hebrew school? How could you possibly debate this Jesuit champion?"

"Yes, I know," replied the usually excessively humble but now surprisingly confident Berl, "I did not finish the second year of *cheder,* but I feel that I can do this."

The elders had a new quandary, another real moral problem. To accept Berl's self-nomination would be to send him to his death. But if not Berl, then who? No one from the village had a chance to prevail in any scholarly debate, and certainly not against such a fierce warrior-scholar as the priest promised to be. And if they sent no one, then the prince's minions would descend upon them all. Finally, after much discussion and even more weeping, they drew upon what little knowledge they had of Jewish law and the greater knowledge they took from fatalistic common sense and agreed that Berl would go. He assumed the task with modest pride.

On the appointed day the entire village went with Berl to the palace of the prince. There they discovered that the formal apparatus of the debate was already in place. At the head of the large hall stood a great wooden chair in which sat the prince. Ahead of him and to his right was a small table, and behind the table sat the Jesuit theologian. Ahead of the prince and to his left was another table with a chair behind it meant for Berl. Between the two debaters' tables stood a giant man, the prince's chief huntsman, and he leaned upon his immense ax.

The sight terrified the villagers and they set up a hushed wailing as they took their positions, standing, at the rear of the hall. Berl went to the chair behind his table.

The prince ordered the debate to begin. Customarily these debates begin with the flipping of a zloty coin, or some similar lot-casting, in order to decide who will ask the first question; but the priest saw at once that his opponent was a thoroughly unlearned man who could not possibly know any serious theology, and even so, the priest believed so firmly in the intellectual triumph of Christianity that he was sure he would prevail over any Jew who debated him, and so he said that he would give to the Jew the chance to ask the first question.

Berl looked into the steely eyes of his opponent and in a small, barely audible voice said, "What does this mean?—'*Ani lo yodea*'?"

Perhaps you do not know what this means, but the Jesuit priest was a master of biblical languages and many other languages as well, and of course he knew that this Hebrew sentence means 'I do not know', and he said at once, "I do not know."

Alas for the priest, the axman knew no Hebrew, and when he heard "I do not know," he enforced the penalty for not knowing the answer to a question, and in a flash the head of the finest Christian theologian in all that part of Europe lay at the feet of the prince.

The prince was aghast. The assembled people, Jews and Christians, were stunned. When the Jews had recovered they ran to the front of the room, hoisted Berl to their shoulders, and made their way home to their village as fast as they could.

Once at home they went directly to the synagogue and offered countless prayers, including one improvised for the occasion, "Words of thanksgiving from those recently delivered from Jesuit theology." Afterward they repaired to the largest room in the village, in the study house, where they drank a little and sang and danced and congratulated Berl endlessly, always complimenting him on the immense subtlety of his question.

At last one of the villagers had celebrated long enough for his curiosity and courage to rise, and he approached Berl, saying, "Berl, you are a great man and your name will live forever; but I would like to ask you, master of the theological interrogation: how did you, a man who never passed through even the second year of *cheder*, how did you think of such a magnificent question?"

"It is true," said Berl, "that I completed but one year of *cheder*, but it was in *cheder* I learned that which saved us today. During that first year, one day the *cheder* was visited by a very famous man. It was Rabbi Weinstein, from Berlin, who was making a visit to our village to see an old aunt of his. The famous Rabbi Weinstein, the greatest scholar and teacher in Berlin, paid a brief visit to the *cheder*. When he stopped by me I was trying to read my Hebrew text. There was a sentence I could not translate, and so I said to the great scholar, "Rabbi Weinstein, please, what does this mean—'*Ani lo yodea*'? And he said, "I do not know." Today I thought, if even Rabbi

Weinstein didn't know, then surely this Jesuit priest does not know."[39]

PAGE 42 Two rabbis and the corpse of a Chinese man. The reference is to a fine poem of Robert Pinsky's, "Impossible to Tell," printed in his collection *The Figured Wheel* (New York: Farrar, Straus and Giroux, 1996).

Since I first began thinking about jokes, I have thought that jokes are significantly like works of art, and although I have not taken up that matter much in this book, I have mentioned it from time to time. When I was asked to speak about jokes and death (a few years ago, by the Illinois Humanities Council), I happened to be reading Robert Pinsky's poems and was working on "Impossible to Tell." It was a striking, lucky congruence. Pinsky's poem is a work of high art. It is essentially a kind of elegy for his lost friend, and in the course of the poem Pinsky recounts the creation of a joke. Art, jokes, and death—all together.

PAGE 66 Why should 'eretz' be spelled with a gimmel?
'Eretz' is a Hebrew word meaning, roughly, land (as in "land of Israel"). Gimmel is the third letter of the Hebrew alphabet. 'Eretz' is not spelled with a gimmel. (Why should it be?)

PAGE 68 In the story about the *apikoros*, '*apikoros*' means an Epicurean, a skeptic, someone outside the faith who may be a danger to subvert it; *treif* is food that is not kosher; the *siddur* is the schedule of regular prayers and observances; and, of course, a goy is a non-Jew.

39. This masterpiece was told to me by a master teller, the late Manny Goldman, a man of great wit equaled by his wisdom and kindness.

INDEX OF JOKES BY FIRST LINE, PUNCH LINE, AND SUBJECT